OUT OF THIS KITCHEN

a History of the Ethnic Groups and Their Foods in the Steel Valley

SECOND EDITION

PUBLASSIST

Pittsburgh, Pennsylvania

CREDITS

*The contents of this book have been produced as a collaborative effort.
We wish to thank the following individuals and organizations who have
contributed to the production of this book:*

Conception, Editor, Dan Karaczun

Book Designer, Jo Butz

Writer, Michelle Fanzo

Food Editor, Contributing Writer, Research, Adele Vamos

Marketing and Distribution, James Hughes

Photo Archives, Randolph Harris, Russ Gibbons

Photography, Steve Swingenstein, Dan Karaczun

Typesetting, Layout, Joanne and Dan Karaczun

Graphics, Production and Pre-press, Publassist

Printing, Chas. M. Henry Printing Company

*The first edition of "Out of This Kitchen" was funded in part by the Steel
Industry Heritage Corporation, dedicated to preserving the industrial
history of the Steel Valley.*

*Special thanks to the people of the Steel Valley for their valuable recipes,
heritage and support. Many of the recipes haven't been written down until
now, and the time and effort involved in organizing them was substantial.
Some of our contributors were kind enough to prepare the dish before sending us the recipe, to ensure that the measurements — which up to that point
were done by eye — would accurately reflect and preserve the rich culture of
the Steel Valley. However, the recipes were not tested by us.*

*Partial proceeds from the sale of this book will be contributed to the
Rainbow Kitchen and the Mon Valley Food Bank.*

TABLE OF CONTENTS

Rendering of Homestead, PA 1902 from an elevated view. Photo courtesy Randolph Harris.

INTRODUCTION

Seventeen years, seven months and twenty-four days of working swing shifts during freezing nights, hot days, Christmas, Easter and Labor Day. But, I didn't walk away with nothing.

During the almost eighteen years I got something that few people in the world could get. I met some of the most interesting and dedicated workers anywhere. I learned about the families and their hopes for their children. I also learned what they wanted to do with their retirement years and how they fit into the big picture. I learned that in spite of working with old machinery and outdated technology that they still made some of the best steel in the world. I learned about the courage and dedication that made the Homestead Works unique in the world steel economy.

For over one hundred years these people and their ancestors toiled in the most unwelcome conditions to care for their families by contributing their labor to the nation's steel industry. Labor that made the United States the greatest industrial power in the world.

1992 marked the centennial celebration of the great "Homestead Massacre." A time when the locked-out steel workers attempted to defend their right to collective bargaining, good wages and decent working conditions by preventing the Pinkertons, hired by Henry Clay Frick, from landing on the banks of the Monongahela at the Homestead Works. This singular act would change the relationship between management and labor forever. No longer would labor take for granted that their bosses were benefactors and no longer would industrial giants take for granted the passiveness of labor.

Historians by the dozens have written and are continuing to write about the events that led up to the "Massacre" and its consequences. Some have said that the steel workers had every right to defend their incomes and others maintain that the company had a right to protect their property from union vandalism and hooliganism. The only thing that we intend to say by publishing this book is that the people who made up the communities of Homestead, Munhall, West Homestead, Hays and later Homestead Park, West Mifflin, Rankin, Braddock and Swissvale were good, honest people regardless of race or national origin.

All American citizens, with the exception of the native Indian population, are immigrants. Although some Americans resist the idea of the melting pot beyond white, anglo-American Protestantism, the fact remains that we are a melting pot with peoples of different religious persuasions, cultural heritage and racial origins. Although these traits are by definition differences, we continually erase these lines of difference as time passes. We melt our differences into one common culture by intermarriage and proximity to other communities and groups. Still one element of culture unites us all beyond all others, our need for and enjoyment of food. What better way is there to celebrate the history of the valley and its people than by making the family meal itself a celebration.

This book is not a celebration of steel, the company, or the union. It is a celebration of the people of the valley and their cultures through food, the most common element of culture. Steel and its manufacture are the unifying elements, the reasons why all of these people came together.

As we investigated the different communities that compose the valley's population, we found that migration to the valley followed the events of world and U.S. history. In the eighteenth century, first the Germans followed by English settled the valley and began farming the hills and valleys. Later, in the early nineteenth century the Scotch-Irish settled into the farms and centers of population and with the earlier settlers formed villages and towns. The appearance of Andrew Carnegie and the needs of the Carnegie Illinois Steel Company brought new labor to the valley in the latter half of the century. The Huns, (Hungarians, Czechs and Slovaks, people from the Austro-Hungarian Empire) brought with them the traditions and recipes of their homeland. Other Slavs, Russians, Ukrainians, Bulgarians and Macedonians also migrated to the valley. All of these latter immigrants of the nineteenth and early twentieth centuries were attempting to escape adverse economic and political conditions in their homelands. The Blacks, Italians and others brought with them the various aspects of their cultures to the unity of the mills and the melting pot of the industrial revolution.

Our intentions were to include all peoples who worked in the Homestead mills and their cultures in this book. However, we could not. Instead we concentrated on the largest of these populations for expediency. Although there is a large concentration of Croatians and Serbians in the Pittsburgh vicinity, they did not make up a significant portion of the population around the Homestead mills. The Spanish settled in Charleroi, the Croatians and Serbs in Ambridge and Aliquippa. In fact the majority of Hungarians settled in Duquesne and McKeesport but managed to get enough representation in the Homestead-Munhall area to be included in this book. We promise to do other books about other steel towns and will include these ethnic groups in them where appropriate.

We begin each section with a brief historical reference to place the events of world and national history within the lives of the people and their conditions. Next, we tell the story of a family or individual from one of the ethnic groups to create a local reference point. Finally, we move to the central purpose of this book, the food.

ICONS

The use of the "schoolhouse" icon is for students to commemorate the steel workers of 1892 and the various ethnic groups of their origin. Although our research could not find a definite link between family income and diet, we feel that planning a menu from "rich" to "lean" during the strike period from July 1st through November 30 will bring to mind the sacrifices made by the steel workers and their families as a result of lost income. This will enable students to experience first hand the trauma associated with America's history of "Strikes" and "Lockouts."

We have used the "Lunchpail" icon to determine a recipe that was either taken to the mill for lunch or that would lend itself to that use. Often, leftovers served this purpose.

The best steel labor in the world exists in Homestead and currently sits idle. Some still look for new employment while others have lost hope and others have found new jobs or small business to replace their lost income. The tragedy is the result of the failure of our business leaders and our government to adjust to changing economic times in a world economy, while some of our business leaders and government officials, frankly, have sold us out for their own benefit. Some say that this is the American way, the rest of us know better.

In over one hundred years in the history of the mills, we have forgotten or ignored the experience gained by that history. Today, in Detroit, Cleveland, Peoria and other cities in America's great Northeast, the confrontation between ownership and employment still exists. And, the vital basic industries of our economy are moving to other parts of the world where labor is cheap and there are no child labor laws. Eventually the third world labor market will awaken and we will all compete and cooperate on an equal footing. But, how many families must suffer the experience of the steel workers in this valley before all people enjoy the right to a decent wage and a bright future for their children, a future free from the anticipation of deprivation and suffering. When will the people who wrest control of industry become mentors and teachers rather than masters.

So, lets sit down and break some bread among us all. The Slovaks and Blacks, the Hungarians and Russians, the Ukrainians and Italians, the Bulgarians and Macedonians, the Scotch/Irish, the Germans and English. In fact lets all lift a cup to our common humanity and break bread, no matter what our origin. We are all Americans, citizens of the World and masters of our future, if we dare to take up the challenge to care about one another.

Daniel A. Karaczun, Editor

LABOR UNREST
AND THE HOMESTEAD STRIKE OF 1892

Pittsburgh became an economic, rather than social or civic, entity early in its history. The unique combination of natural waterways, diverse topography and bucolic greenery which first attracted agrarian settlers from the east, were quickly recognized as ideal for transportation, building and trading as the region rapidly emerged as the gateway to the West for thousands of ambitious pioneers.

Natural resources and the demand for blacksmiths in a burgeoning society — to produce such necessities as horseshoes, nails and axes — were the impetus for Pittsburgh's first manufacturing industry, and its first pseudonym, Iron City. Easterners and immigrants made up the labor force for the iron, glass, metals and textile industries in the early part of the 19th century — a remarkably harmonious time for labor-management relations in western Pennsylvania.

The paternalistic attitude of industry leaders — providing housing, hunting rights and gardens for workers — changed in the late 1850s when coke production prompted a move from country to city based workplaces, where there was better transportation and a more readily available labor pool. Molders protesting a wage cut in 1842 marked the first area strike. They lost, but three years later boilers and puddlers won their grievance against wage reduction.

The success of this united effort between boilers and puddlers may have spurred the massive shift from small craft group unionization to almost universal unionization by 1850. Boilers, heaters, refiners, scrappers and puddlers walked off the job united that year to discover their protest produced the importation of strikebreakers, and the loss of their livelihood. The Sons of Vulcan, a secret society of boilers and puddlers formed in 1858, remained underground until the Civil War ended the industry's depression. The Grand Forge of the United States, United Sons of Vulcan emerged in 1862 and spread rapidly to seven other states.

Numerous post-Civil War strikes led to a sliding scale agreement between labor and industry in 1867. Peace reigned until a spate of lock-outs and strikes seven years later. 1875 saw the significant formation of the Amalgamated Association of Iron and Steel Workers from the merger of three craft unions, with the Sons of Vulcan dominating with 85 percent of its membership.

It only took a few years before union-management relations soured again in the late 1870s, a period marred by strikes and firings primarily attributed to the increasing mechanization of the steel industry. The union's membership continued to mount rapidly through the 1880s, mushrooming from 11,800 in 1883 to a peak of 24,000 eight years later.

Then came the event no one had predicted but every labor dispute had foreshadowed: the devastating Homestead Steel Strike of 1892.

View of Homestead from Squirrel Hill circa 1890.

THE HOMESTEAD STEEL STRIKE OF 1892

By 1892 the division between Prince and Pauper clearly reflected the differences between wealthy industry magnates and the immigrant work force. The absolute power of the employer had placed workers at a disadvantage in spite of established unions like the Amalgamated. By the end of the nineteenth century, a handful of employers controlled Pittsburgh, and the lives of its labor force.

Workers were being paid as little as possible while being expected to work as hard as possible. The fairness of working conditions, wages, and hours was not a major concern of the employer. A natural animosity developed between unions and employers, feeding the flames for an inevitable conflict that would transcend international boundaries.

Homestead, located on the Monongahela River near many bountiful bituminous coal mines, possessed all the elements necessary to become the singular place it was — the world's premiere steel town. The development of 600 acres of riverfront property in 1880 prompted massive development in the town, boasting a population increase from 600 at the time of construction to 8,000 at the time of the strike.

In 1892 Andrew Carnegie was spending the summer in his native Scotland, leaving Henry Clay Frick in charge of the Homestead Works at the time a new contract was being negotiated for workers. Frick announced a decrease in wage would have to be accepted or non-union workers would be brought in to fill the men's jobs.

While negotiations were breaking off and departments were being shut down, Frick constructed "Fort Frick," a three mile wooden fence topped with barbed wire and observation outlooks that surrounded the mill site. Part of the allure of the Homestead land had been "the ease with which the mill property could be equipped for offensive and defensive purposes, because the ruin wrought in that town by a disastrous strike would be more sweeping and complete than could be effected anywhere else, and because the Carnegie Company had the largest interests to serve and should, therefore, be willing to bear the brunt of the battle," wrote Pittsburgh journalist Arthur Burgoyne in 1893 in *The Homestead Strike of 1892.*

What followed was a 143 day strike that changed labor relations nationally for four decades. On July 6, 1892, 300 armed Pinkerton men hired by Frick to protect non-union workers arrived by barge in front of the mill. In the clash that ensued it was never determined who fired first, but four Pinkertons and seven millworkers lay dead by sundown. An unappeased mob tried to destroy the barges, frightening the Pinkertons into surrender. Before they were allowed to leave Homestead, the Pinkertons were severely pummeled by a riotous mob and their barges destroyed. Eighty-five hundred of the state's National Guard were called in to take control of the site back from the irate crowd.

Workers in three other Carnegie mills showed solidarity with their fellow laborers by also walking out. It became apparent to the country as well as area millworkers that what was happening in Homestead was a symbol of organized labor fighting industry management everywhere, and would permanently alter labor relations in America.

Public sympathy stayed with the strike leaders until a nervous, young revolutionary, Alexander Berkman, tried to assassinate Frick for reasons unrelated to the strike. Berkman's failed effort placed him in jail for 22 years while winning support for what the public

Paylines: Photo courtesy Randolph Harris

The Main Gate: Photo courtesy Randolph Harris

Overlooking the Main Gate: Photo courtesy Randolph Harris

perceived as the brave Frick. By this time the mill had begun production with strikebreakers and on November 20, 1892, what was left of the union gave up.

Many strikers returned to work, but for lower pay, longer hours and no contract. The Amalgamated lost power and membership into the turn of the twentieth century. After a failed strike in 1903, it would be thirty-four years before a union would again be a viable organization in any major steel mill in Pennsylvania.

Ironically, labor unions regained their strength just before World War II, a mere two decades before workers' jobs would again be threatened by an entity that strikes, negotiations and compromises could never address — the national economic decline of the steel industry.

THE FORT THAT FRICK BUILT

Twixt Homestead and Munhall,
If you'll believe my word at all
Where once a steel works noisy roar
A thousand blastings did out-pour
There stands today with great pretense
Enclosed with a white-washed fence
O wonderous change of great import
The mills transformed into a fort.
Anonymous
Homestead Local News, July 2, 1892

ENDED! DEFEAT ACKNOWLEDGED AFTER FOUR-AND-A-HALF MONTHS OF BITTER CONFLICT

To-day marks the closing scenes of the great Homestead strike. It is now virtually at an end. For a month or more it has been apparent that the workmen could not win and a prolongation of the strike was simply a useless sacrifice. This however was not acknowledged by the larger number, and they held out against fate. During the week a great change in the attitude of the strikers has taken place, and the conclusion seems to have been forced upon them, that they must save themselves. Although several meetings were held by both the Amalgamated lodges and the mechanics and laborers, nothing was offered to encourage them to continue the fight. The Hungarian and Slav workmen, were the first to break away, and on Thursday afternoon rushed in a body to the mill office to secure their jobs. There were about 300 of them and half the number were given employment at once and the remainder were promised work sooner or later. This break was the forerunner of a larger and more important one yesterday afternoon, which included the English speaking laborers and the mechanics, together with a limited number of the Amalgamated men.

Over one thousand workmen applied for their jobs. They were given passes to enter the mill and directed to the various foremen of the different departments. In many instances, especially among the laboring classes, work was secured, but in other cases the old workmen found their jobs in other hands and were turned away. Probably three hundred obtained work. A large number, however, were promised employment in a few days, or as soon as an opening should occur. There were a few though that were denied work under any circumstances, as they were objectionable to the company for obvious reasons. They turned away with a sorry tread. The majority of those breaking away are what is known as sympathy strikers. So far as they are concerned the strike is off. Not so with the Amalgamated men. It is not the policy of the association to end a strike in this manner. Even though the struggle is in all respects ended, still it is not declared off officially.

Homestead Local News, November 19, 1892

INTRODUCTION TO EARLY RECIPES

When Jane Nespoli* of Swissvale wanted to learn how to cook like her Irish grandmother, she watched the preparation of food with keen interest. Two handfuls of flour, a pinch of salt, a blop of honey…the precise science of cooking was once a much more organic endeavor. "You put in what feels right to your hand," Jane recalls her grandmother saying. The young girl's palm measured differently than her grandmother's, generating difficulties she soon outgrew.

The time when families begin writing down the amount of a recipe's ingredients is different for each, some never do so. (I remember my Italian grandmother giving me her set of measuring spoons to play "tea party" with because she had no use for them.) A few of the earlier entries published in *Out of This Kitchen* are characteristic of that more individual style. Imprecise amounts, curious kitchen aids (where can a canton-flannel cloth be found?), and peculiar terminology occasionally appear in the older recipes, dating as far back as 1756. Adjust them to your present resources, and if you run into something you aren't sure of (just how big is "half a crown"?), do what Jane does — see what feels right.

*From an interview with Jane Nespoli for the Steel Industry Heritage Corporation's ethnographic survey of the Mon Valley.

TO MAKE LITTLE CAKES FOR TEA
MOTHER BUCK

This recipe dates back to 1756!

Of butter, flour, sugar, a quarter of a pound of each and as much yolk of egg as will mix into a stiff paste. Make them into round cakes the size of half a crown. Bake them in tins. Put some caraway seeds in them.

Adele Buck, Penn Hills

HOW TO MAKE AN OMELET

"If it were my privilege to examine all the cooks in the city," says Mrs. Rover, "I should first put them to making omelets, as nothing would betray more quickly the skill or ignorance of a cook than the handling of the breakfast omelet." And then she explains how it should be made.

Have an omelet pan about eight inches in diameter — one made from sheet iron preferable. The bottom should be as smooth as glass. If not, put into it a teaspoonful of salt, and then with a piece of brown paper scour it thoroughly. Do not wash it after, simply turn the salt out and put in a piece of butter the size of a walnut. Break four to six eggs into a bowl, and with a fork give twelve to fifteen vigorous beats, not enough to make the mixture light, but to thoroughly mix the white and the yolks of the eggs. Beating either together or separately robs eggs of their flavor, and also makes small air cells, which expand as the pan is heated and cool as the omelet is turned over for the table, thus making a heavy rather than a light and tender one. Do not add salt or pepper to the omelet until it is nearly done. Salt toughens the eggs. Add one teaspoonful of boiling water to each egg as soon as they are beaten. Put in a piece of butter the size of a hickory nut. Now put the frying pan over the fire having already placed in it a piece of butter the size of a walnut, and as soon as it is melted, not brown, pour in the eggs. Place over a quick fire, shake as soon as the omelet begins to have a set appearance; with a limber knife lift the eggs, allowing the more liquid part to go underneath, thus forming layers, as it were, being very careful not to tear the omelet, or it will have the appearance of scrambled eggs. Now sprinkle the omelet with salt and pepper, and continue lifting until the whole has been put in a jelly-like condition. If the pan is perfectly smooth the omelet will not stick. When done and set, not hard, slip a knife under the omelet — that part next to the handle of the pan — roll it over, then turn gently on to a heated dish; serve at once. It is better that you should wait five minutes for your omelet than that your omelet should wait one minute for you.

You will notice I have used water in preference to milk. Milk contains a small amount of cheese, toughens in cooking and spoils the omelet. Neither should you use thickening of any kind — cornstarch or flour. Simply take the egg and water and you will have a tender, delicious omelet. One more caution, the omelet should not be a dark brown, as it destroys the flavor of the egg.

Homestead Local News, January 26, 1894

POTATO COOKERY

It seems a pity to the New York World that when there are so many delicious ways of serving potatoes, they are ever sent to the table in the unappetizing lump form which is most prevalent. Here are a few substitutes for the everlasting "boiled" potato.

Potatoes in Jackets — Bake as many potatoes as are needed. Cut a small piece from one end and a larger one from the other. Remove the inside and rub through a sieve. Put on the fire with half an ounce of butter and one ounce of grated cheese for every four potatoes. Add boiling milk, salt and pepper as for mashed potatoes. Fill the skins with this paste, sprinkle tops with grated bread crumbs and cheese and put in the oven to brown.

Potato Souffle — Boil six good-sized mealy potatoes. Rub through a sieve. Scald a teacup of sweet milk and three teaspoons of butter. Add one at a time the well-beaten yolks of six eggs. Beat the whites to a froth and stir lightly into the mixture. Pour into a well-buttered baking dish and bake for about half an hour in a quick oven.

Potato Balls — Mash some potatoes with salt, pepper, butter and a little chopped parsley. Roll into balls, dip in beaten egg, roll in bread crumbs and fry for a few minutes in hot butter.

Texas Baked Potatoes — Mash and season with pepper and salt some good Irish potatoes. Mince a large onion fine, mix thoroughly with the potatoes and bake in a brisk oven.

Homestead Local News, February 15, 1894

100 Years Ago
The largest nickel-steel ingot ever made in the country — 18 inches thick — was cast at the Homestead steel mill's No. 2 open hearth. It would be rolled into armor plate for the USS Monterey.
Pittsburgh Press, April 24, 1992

If, after brushing the coat or gown, it is sprinkled with spirits of camphor and aired a few hours, it will be tidy and graceful. Garments and belongings that smell of nothing are the cleanest and most agreeable.
Homestead Local News, January 25, 1894

SAMP OR HOMINY

Soak a pint of dried hulled corn over night in enough cold water to cover it, and in the morning put over the fire in the same water and boil it gently for about four hours, or until it is tender; a very little salt may be added just before it is done; when the samp is tender drain it; either heat it with a palatable seasoning of salt, pepper and butter and serve it hot, or rub it dry on a clean towel, and fry it as follows: put in a frying-pan over the fire two heaping teaspoonfuls of lard or drippings, for a pint of boiled samp, and fry it light brown; stir it occasionally to insure equal cooking, and when it is done season it with salt and pepper and serve it as a vegetable.

Homestead Local News, January 31, 1894

POTATO ROULETTES

Mix a pint mashed potatoes with a tablespoonful of cream, salt and pepper to season, and the beaten yolk of an egg. Form into oblong roulettes, dip in beaten egg, roll in bread crumbs and fry in hot lard to a golden brown.

Homestead Local News, December 22, 1893

FRIED ONIONS

The art of frying an onion so that it will be delicate and crisp is not generally understood. There is but one way to fry this vegetable which will give the right result, that is, to cut it in slices and soak them in milk for at least ten minutes. Then dip the slices in flour and immerse then in boiling fat, hot enough to brown instantly a bit of bread thrown in. You cannot keep the onion in slices, so it is not worth while to try to do so. After they have fried for six or seven minutes they may be lifted up with a skimmer on to brown paper and will be found firm and thor-oughly delicious. Cooked in this way they may be served as a garnish to a daintily-broiled beefsteak or to a dish of fried chops or beef cro-quettes. There is no way of frying an onion in a pan with a little butter, as commonly recommended in cookbooks, which will produce a satis-factory result. The onion softens and absorbs the butter, owing to the natural law of capillary attraction, and the result is that the butter and onion become a dark and greasy mass.

Homestead Local News, January 15, 1894

A can of fresh canned salmon is a luxury in more than one respect as it lends itself so easily to different uses. In the summer it is one of the most convenient things to keep in the house. Its preparation into different dishes being so readily and easily accomplished.
Homestead Local News, July 2, 1892

STEWED CELERY

Scrape and wash one or two heads of celery, cut the stalks into 2 inch lengths and boil half an hour, or until tender, in salted water. Drain off the water, pour over the celery sufficient cream sauce to cover, simmer a few moments and serve.

Homestead Local News, January 15, 1894

SALMON AU GRATIN

Take a coffee cup of salmon free from the liquor, and flake it, mix with it a half cup of cold drawn butter, pepper and salt. Fill a small baking dish with the mixture, cover with fine bread crumbs and brown in the oven. A little mashed potato and half a cup of cream form a nice addition to this dish. It should be served hot and garnished with a little fried parsley. This quantity will serve four people.

SALMON ON TOAST

Flake the fish, season with pepper and salt and heat it with a little milk or cream. Have some hot milk in a flat pan. Toast several slices of bread, dip quickly into the hot milk, place on a hot dish, spread with butter and pour over the heated fish.

SALMON SALAD

One cup of cold salmon minced and mixed with an equal quantity of chopped celery. Line a dish with lettuce leaves, turn into it the mixed salmon and celery, and over all pour a dressing made of two tablespoonfuls of oil, three tablespoonfuls of vinegar, salt and pepper. A mayonnaise dressing may be used, but with salmon, the plain dressing is to be preferred.

Tea and coffee often leave a brown rim around the bottom of cups and saucers. This discoloration can be removed by scouring with salt that has been a little dampened.
Homestead Local News, January 31, 1894

Specialists on throat diseases are beginning to take unusual interest in culinary methods. They advise a kitchen quarantine on wash days and boiled dinner days, giving as a reason that the steam from boiling clothes and pickled meats that require much heat produces many illnesses of the respiratory organs and aggravates slight or chronic diseases of the nose, throat and lungs. Patients are advised to vacate apartments having dark or ill-ventilated kitchens and to keep all babies and ailing children out of the kitchen when cooking is going on.
This comment, originally published in the Pittsburgh Dispatch, ran in the Household Affairs column of the January 29, 1894, Homestead Local News.

CHICKEN PIE

Cut up a fat fowl in quite small pieces. The leg and second joint may be made into two pieces each by cutting as large a piece as possible from the fleshy side of each. The wings are to be separated at the second joint. Large pieces may be cut from the breast, and the back can be broken with a stroke of a hammer and cut in two. Take half a pound of fat pork and cut in small pieces. Put these on in water to just cover and cook until done. Take off to cool. Make a paste with 1 quart of flour, 1 teaspoon of soda, 2 teaspoons of cream of tartar, 1 teaspoon salt, 1 coffee cup shortening, all butter or half lard. Work them together and use milk enough to make as soft a paste as you can roll out. Take half the quantity and roll out until one-third of an inch thick and line the side of your pan, letting it come an inch above the bottom and the same above the top.

Now put in the contents of the saucepan, which have already been seasoned with salt alone. If more gravy is needed, put in water to suit. Stir up a large tablespoonful of flour smoothly with milk and add. Then dredge the whole with flour and lay on the top crust, which must be half an inch longer than the pan. Roll the side crust being sure it is perfectly tight. Then press your thumb down into this edge at intervals of an inch. Bake until the crust is done — not too dark brown and you have a dish fit for a king.

Homestead Local News, February 15, 1893

In boiling chickens for salad put them to cook in cold water and let them come slowly to the boiling point. This process makes them more tender and blanches the dark meat — usually rejected — so it may be mixed with the white. The dressing should not be added to the salad until serving time. If mixed long before serving it becomes watery.
Homestead Local News, December 15, 1893

Buy bar soap by the quantity of you wish to be truly economical. Stand these bars on edge, one above another, with as much open space as possible between them. They will then dry out and last almost twice as long.
Homestead Local News, July 2, 1892

SCALLOPED OYSTERS

Butter a deep pan or baking dish, cover the bottom with rolled crackers or bread crumbs slightly toasted. Over this put a layer of oysters seasoned with pepper and salt and a little butter, then another layer of crumbs and one more of oysters, salt, pepper and butter. The top layer should be of crumbs seasoned with pepper and salt. Over this put small pieces of butter. Bake about half an hour.

Homestead Local News, December 22, 1893

CORN-FRITTERS

For corn fritters, either cooked or raw corn may be used. With four eggs eight ears of corn are necessary. A chopping-knife can be used advantageously to remove the corn from the cob, as the work can be done in much less time than with a knife. One tablespoonful of sugar, one teaspoonful of salt, one pint of sweet milk, one tablespoonful of melted butter, and three tablespoonfuls of flour are also necessary. Beat the yolks of the eggs smooth, stir the corn in slowly, then sugar and salt, flour, melted butter, milk and last of all, the whites of the eggs beaten into a stiff froth. Heat a griddle, grease it lightly with butter, and drop the batter on in tablespoonfuls. Turn with a cake turner. The fritters must be quickly cooked, and served while very hot.

Homestead Local News, January 31, 1894

DOUGHNUTS IN RHYME

One cup of sugar, one cup of milk;
Two eggs beaten, free as silk.
Salt and nutmeg (lemon'll do);
Of baking powder teaspoons two.
Lightly stir the flour in;
Roll on pie board not too thin.
Cut in diamonds, twists or rings,
Drop with care the doughy things
Into fat that briskly swells
Evenly the sponge cells.
Watch with care the time for turning;
Fry them brown — just short of burning.
Roll in sugar; serve when cool.
Price — a quarter for this rule.

Homestead Local News, January 31, 1894

APPLE DUMPLINGS

Peel, core and cut up six ripe apples. Prepare a rich pastry, take small pieces of it, roll out and cut into slices about the size of a breakfast saucer. Into each put a teaspoonful of butter, two teaspoonfuls of sugar and two or three tablespoonfuls of minced apple. Form into balls by drawing the edges of crust together. Put them in a pan and sprinkle over the top a little sugar and some tiny pieces of butter. Cover with boiling water and bake, adding a little more water if it gets low before the dumplings are done.

Homestead Local News, December 22, 1893

HOW TO MAKE HOMEMADE CAKES

In large cities the making of cake is almost a lost art. There are many reasons for this, first and foremost of which is the bakery. Then there are the women's exchanges, where people fancy they can buy just such cakes as dear grandma used to make, but oh, what a delusion and a snare they prove! "The test of the pudding is in the eating," but the test of bought cakes, either at bakeries or exchanges should be left entirely to their appearance, for there alone is their merit. I have a friend who makes the most delicious cake I ever tasted. One of the best and easiest made of her almost endless variety of cakes is what she calls a:

Luncheon Cake

One cupful of sugar, one-half cup of butter, worked to a fine cream; one egg; one cupful of sweet milk; two cupfuls of flour; three teaspoonfuls of baking powder. Flavor with grated nutmeg. Bake in a shallow pan well lined with buttered paper.

Sometimes she frosts the top of this cake and decorates it with English walnut meats. Then she calls it reception cake. Another of her cakes is what all children love. She calls it:

Sponge Cake

One large cup of sugar, four eggs beaten to a foam, three tablespoonfuls of milk, two teaspoonfuls of baking powder, one large cup of flour, flavor with lemon.

This makes a small cake. It should be baked in a shallow, square pan, and eaten fresh. Another of her cakes is rich and delicious; she calls it:

Wedding Cake

Two pounds of sugar, two pounds of granulated sugar, twelve eggs. Beat whites and yolks separately. One cup of New Orleans molasses, three tablespoonfuls of cloves, one tablespoonful of mace, two tablespoonfuls of allspice, one nutmeg grated, a quarter of a pound of citron cut in little pieces, four pounds of dried currants, two pounds of flour and one heaping teaspoonful of baking soda.

This must be thoroughly beaten and mixed and baked four hours in a slow oven. To frost it beat up the whites of four eggs to a stiff froth, add powdered sugar as long as you can blend it nicely, also add the juice of one lemon. Spread this over the top of the cake nearly an inch thick and around the sides half that thickness.

Here you have a cake fit to set before a king. It will keep for months.

Homestead Local News, February 15, 1893

Flatirons should be kept as far removed from the steam of cooking as possible, as this is what causes them to rust.
Homestead Local News, February 15, 1893

STRAWBERRY SHORT CAKE

This deservedly popular luncheon dish is sure to prove a success if directions are carefully followed. Mix well and rub through a sieve one quart of flour, three teaspoonfuls of baking powder, two tablespoonfuls of granulated sugar and a teaspoonful of salt. Rub into this a scant half-teacupful of nice butter, and mix into a soft dough with a pint of water (measuring a trifle scant). Divide the dough into four equal parts. Have ready two greased baking pans about ten inches square and roll out the dough to fit them, placing two layers in each. Bake about fifteen minutes in a quick oven. The layers can be separated by simply pulling them apart. Have ready three pints of strawberries into which you have lightly chopped a cupful and a half of powdered sugar; chop them in a large earthen bowl, using a common knife; do not mash them. Spread between the layers, forming the four layers into one loaf. Trim off the edges with a very sharp knife, cut into the daintiest of cubes and serve hot, passing a pitcher of whipped cream with it.

Serve strawberries in French style, with their hulls on, arranging them in individual dishes and garnish with some of their delicate leaves, with a strawberry blossom dotted here and there. Pass little shells of powdered sugar with them, or the sugar may be served in tiny Chinese cups placed in the center of the saucer of strawberries. The effect is both unique and exceedingly pretty.

The Local News, June 25, 1892

ORANGE CAKE

2 cups sugar	½ cup water
5 egg yolks	½ tsp. soda
1 orange,	1 tsp. cream tartar
grated rind and juice only	4 egg whites
2 cups flour	

Stir the sugar and yolks together with the orange rind and juice until it is creamed very smooth. Add water, soda and cream tartar and flour. Beat whites and stir in last.

Icing

1 egg white	1 orange,
12 tbls. sugar	grated rind and juice only

Place between the layers of the cake.

Homestead Local News, July 1, 1892

CRANBERRY SAUCE

Wash and pick the berries, removing all imperfect ones. Put them in a porcelain kettle; to a quart of berries allow a pint of sugar. Boil ten or fifteen minutes taking care not to mash the berries. Pour into a deep dish or a mold.

Homestead Local News, December 22, 1893

PUMPKIN PIE

One quart of sieved pumpkin pressed through a sieve, eight eggs beaten separately, two scant quarts of sweet milk, one pint sugar, a teaspoonful each of butter, cinnamon and nutmeg. Beat together and bake in pie pans lined with rich pastry.

Homestead Local News, December 22, 1893

OLD FASHIONED CURRANT DUMPLINGS

Old-fashioned currant dumpling, boiled in a cloth, is seldom seen on our tables, and yet it is generally a favorite, and will be found just the thing to vary the desserts. It is made thus: Into a pint of flour, sifted, with a heaping teaspoonful of salt, rub a large teacupful of finely chopped beef suet and the same of currants, washed thoroughly and dried in a cloth; now with a fork stir into this enough very cold water (about a third of a cupful) to make a rather soft biscuit-like dough. Put this into a floured canton-flannel cloth, rough side out allowing room to swell; tie closely with a stout string and pop it into a potful of boiling water; cook for three hours and do not let the water stop boiling for a moment; replenish from the hot teakettle. It should turn out a light, appetizing ball. Half a cupful of granulated sugar may be rubbed through the flour if liked; if not the soft white sauce should be well sweetened. Flavor the latter with nutmeg or vanilla.

Homestead Local News, January 29, 1894

An old postcard of the Rail Mill in Carnegie, PA. circa 1900.

OYSTER SOUP

To make a delicious soup out of these succulent bivalves observe the following directions: Have two nice agate or porcelain lined saucepans, one for milk and the other for the juice of the oysters. As this is a dinner for eight people you must have good-sized saucepans. Put in one three pints of milk, with a heaping tablespoonful of butter, a level teaspoonful of salt and two blades of mace. Stand over a slow fire. In the other saucepan put the liquor from two quarts of oysters, leaving the oysters in the colander through which the liquor has been drained until ready for use. Stand this over the hot part of the range, and as soon as the scum rises skim every fleck of it off with a silver or agate spoon — iron or other metal should not be used in cooking. After skimming stand the stewpan back where it does not boil; as soon as the milk begins to boil pour the oyster liquor into it, stirring gently to prevent curdling. Have ready two heaping tablespoonfuls of flour, well mixed with cold milk; thicken the soup with this, stirring fast to break the lumps. If it is a bit lumpy strain through a fine colander into the empty stewpan. Put back on the range and when it begins to boil drop the oysters in and let them cook until edges curl. Put some fine chopped parsley and a pinch of powdered cloves in the bottom of the tureen. Pour the soup in, sprinkle in a little black pepper and it is ready to serve.

Homestead Local News, January 31, 1894

The rubber rollers of wringing machines that have become sticky or covered with lint from colored clothes can be cleaned by passing a rag wet with kerosene through them.
Homestead Local News, January 31, 1894

Feather beds or pillows should never be put in the sun, for the heat draws out the oil from the feathers giving them a rancid smell. Air them on a windy day where the sun will not touch them.
Homestead Local News, January 31, 1894

Old paint and varnish may be removed by an emulsion formed of two parts of ammonia shaken up with one part of turpentine. It will soften them so they may easily be scraped off.
Homestead Local News, January 31, 1894

Sandwiches can be made some hours before needed if kept in a cool place snugly covered with a damp cloth. They should be piled closely upon a dish.
Homestead Local News, December 14, 1893

APPLE JELLY

Apple jelly is little regarded because the apple is so common. Nevertheless it is one of our most excellent fruit jellies, and it is a standard dependence of the French cook in the preparation of fruit pies and various other desserts. The French make many delicious compotes of apples. The difference between a compote and a preserve should be carefully noted. A compote is a preparation of fruit put up for immediate use, as we put up cranberries or stew apples; a preserve is a preparation of fruit intended to be used at some distant time, and may usually be kept a twelvemonth or longer. Apple preserves are an absurdity, as apples are found in market all the year round, except in the beginning of summer, when other fruits are in abundance. Apple jelly is best prepared from time to time as it is needed, though there is no objection to having two weeks supplies in the house for fruit pies and general use. A compote should not be made more than a day or two at the farthest before it is to be served. The most familiar American compote, molded cranberries, is considered to be in its prime condition the day after it is made.

For an apple jelly select a dozen firm, well flavored apples. Fall pippins make an excellent jelly, but almost any well flavored, slightly tart apple will do for this purpose. Do not peel the apples, but cut them into quarters, leaving the core in, but removing any wormy specks. Partially decayed apples are unfit for the purpose. Pour a pint of cold water over them and slice in half a lemon. Put them in a porcelain-lined kettle to boil. Let them cook for twenty minutes, and then strain them through a fine sieve or a coarse cloth. Add sugar in the proportions of a pound to every pint of juice. Let the sugar and apple juice boil together for twenty minutes. Then test the mixture, and as soon as it forms a jelly pour it into cups. A layer of this jelly spread over an apple meringue pie before the meringue is put on is a great improvement, and most French cooks use such a layer in all their fruit pies, both next to the crust and over the fruit, so that the fruit is incased in the apple jelly. The reason for this is that the apple is an inexpensive, convenient article to use, and possess the ability to take to itself the flavor of other fruits, like peaches, pineapples and greengages. A most delicate apple meringue pie is made of apple jelly strongly tinctured with lemon juice and covered with a meringue flavored with lemon. For the purpose of economy a nice applesauce, strained as it should be, and with a layer of apple jelly over it and then the layer of meringue is more often used.

Homestead Local News, January 15, 1894

In making lemonade strain the juice, and to improve the taste allow a half dozen oranges to every dozen lemons. If desired a few thin rounds of banana may be added.
Homestead Local News, December 15, 1892

GERMANS

The Germans were the first group of settlers to make Pennsylvania their home, arriving in the state's western region as early as 1708. While Germans, mostly of the lower classes from the oppressed Palatinate (later to become part of Bavaria) arrived between 1708-1728, the following 75 years saw major German immigration for the middle and upper classes, with half the state boasting German roots by 1750. The Germans were frontier people, who moved rapidly from east to west traversing such routes as the Susquehanna, Juniata and Potomac Rivers to make their way over the Allegheny Mountains and into western Pennsylvania.

The first to respond to the state's liberal open-door policy were the German sects of Mennonites, Tunkers, Schwenkfelders, among others, followed by Reformed and Lutheran church members. In general, their rural simplicity — wearing wooden shoes, coarse clothes and toting weapons — was viewed as somewhat crude. The latter church-goers quickly exchanged their language and habits for those of the new land, proving themselves thrifty and industrious people after an initial fear that the massive inrush of Germans was a threat to the colony's very language and government.

As the first settlers of the region, Germans established themselves early on as landlords and shop owners, settling in large numbers in Butler and Armstrong Counties, and the towns of Harmony, Dunkard and Berlin. Pennsylvania German, Louis Thiel, started Thiel College at Greenville in 1865 with a donation to the Evangelical Church.

In 1910 Germans were the largest ethnic group in Pittsburgh, with more than half the 2,400 German millworkers averaging $14.55 a week as skilled or semi-skilled laborers. The twentieth century was an era for Germans to make the headlines, such as Henry Buhl, Jr., Henry Clay Frick, Charles M. Schwab, President of the Carnegie Steel Company, and a number of company presidents, political figures and notable educators.

INTERVIEW

Elmer Best, West Mifflin

Elmer Best was 17 when he lied about his age to get a job at U.S. Steel's Homestead Works as a carpenter in 1924. He worked steady daylight shifts Monday through Saturday — 62 hours a week. "In the winter I never saw my home in the daylight, only on Sundays," he recalls.

Elmer, of German descent, lives in West Mifflin with his wife of 56 years, Mildred. He remembers carrying his "standard" two or three ham sandwiches wrapped in a newspaper for lunch every day. "I never took fruit ... it just wasn't there."

The Homestead Works provided a cafeteria for its employees, but few millworkers could eat there because of the walking distance involved. "That was quite a walk, and you only had a half-hour," Elmer remembers. "I know for sure the cafeteria was there in 1929. It was located near the main gate that we millworkers called 'the whole in the wall'."

Hogs were butchered in the fall on his family's 32-acre farm in West Mifflin, then hung for "eternity" in a smokehouse for curing. His mother baked bread once a week in an outside oven which still stands today, next to the barn's cornerstone marker dated May 1877.

Dinners were "just like the sun rose and set — the same every day," says Elmer. "On Sundays we had roast beef or pork. Desserts and stuff were absolutely unheard of." At his wife's prodding, however, Elmer concedes that his family had a freezer and made ice cream in the summer.

The family's daily breakfast included eggs, sausage and rolled oats. "We didn't have the variety or selection of foods. We had the same thing day in and day out," says Elmer.

Elmer grew up selling vegetables grown on their farm from a horse-drawn wagon in Duquesne, which "looks the same today as it did then." He took one day a week from school during the fall to travel house-to-house, building a clientele.

MEAT STUFFING
(FOR TURKEY)

1 lb. ground sirloin   ½ large loaf of day-old bread

Should be somewhat hard, soaked in enough water to moisten. Squeeze out all water and add to meat. Add:

½ tsp. pepper   1 small onion, grated

1 tsp. salt

Sprinkle:

1 tbl. flour

Mix together and stuff bird.

Barbara Best Starrett

"This recipe has been in our family for 100 years. Grandma Best never used a cook book. This was a favorite, but when her daughter-in-law, Mildred Ritzel Best, asked for the recipe Grandma always changed it a little here or there. No one knows if this was done on purpose or not! Mildred has approximated the meat stuffing as much as possible for her daughter, Barbara Best Starrett. Regardless, everyone knows it can never taste as good as Grandma's!"

GERMAN HOLIDAY BREAD

In the evening set a sponge as usual for bread, in quantity enough for three loaves. In the morning, when fully risen, add one pound of brown sugar, one pint of dried apples or pears, minced fine, one pint of broken hickory or walnut meats, three tablespoonfuls of caraway and one of coriander seeds. Mix thoroughly, mold into loaves and bake when light. Wrap each loaf in a towel and put in a cool place. It will keep for several weeks.

Homestead Local News, January 29, 1894

CORN PUDDING

1 can corn   1 tsp. salt

3 egg yolks, beaten   4 tbls. butter, melted

1 tbl. sugar   3 egg whites

1 tbl. cornstarch

Combine first 6 ingredients. Beat egg whites and fold into mixture. Place in greased baking dish and bake in 350° oven for 30 to 35 minutes.

Adele Buck, Penn Hills

RED LENTIL SOUP

1   8 oz. package dried red
    lentils

3   onions, coarsely chopped

5   cups water

1   bay leaf

1   large clove garlic,
    finely chopped

1   tsp. dried thyme
    or 1 tbls. chopped fresh

3   carrots,
    scraped and thinly sliced

3   tbls. parsley, chopped

    salt and pepper

Wash and drain lentils. In large saucepan combine lentils, onions, water, bay leaf and garlic. Cover and simmer for one hour. Add thyme and carrots. Cover and simmer for 30 minutes. Remove bay leaf. Add parsley, salt and pepper to taste. Serve hot. Makes 8 ¾ cup servings.

Barbara Sturms, Duquesne

GERMAN POTATO BALLS

1 ½ loaves white bread,
     dried and cubed

5   lbs. grated potatoes

2   eggs
     salt and pepper

1   small onion, grated

Mold ingredients into snowball size (will be soupy) and roll in flour. Keep patting to snowball shape. Drop in boiling water; balls will rise to top. Cook 20 minutes. Lift with slotted spoon. Serve with sauerkraut. Makes 20 balls.

Ruth Ann Parkinson, West Mifflin

SOUR MEAT

1   lb. round steak

1 ½ cups water

3   large onions, thinly sliced

flour (for gravy)

2   tbls. white vinegar (more for
     heavier sour taste)

Cut steak into small cubed pieces. Brown meat in 1 tbl. oil. Once meat is browned, add water, onions and vinegar. Cover and simmer until meat and onions are tender (about 1 ½ hours). Continue to add water if needed.

Just before meat is done, prepare a mixture of flour and water. Stir flour mixture and vinegar directly into the skillet and heat thoroughly. Serves 4.

Gert Senich, West Mifflin

BEEF OR VENISON SAUERBRATEN

Marinade

2 cups dry red wine	1 ¾ lbs. beef or venison sirloin
1 stalk celery, minced	2 tbls. butter
1 carrot, finely chopped	½ tbls. all-purpose flour
1 red onion, chopped	1-2 tbls. butter, softened
1 bay leaf	½ cup sour cream
2 tbls. whole black peppercorns	
1 tsp. salt	
¼ tsp. dried thyme	

Combine first 8 marinade ingredients in container large enough to hold meat, mixing well. Wash meat and carefully trim off all visible fat. Put meat in marinade, turning to coat all sides. Refrigerate for 3 days, turning each morning and evening. Remove roast and pat dry. Strain marinade and reserve. In large skillet, brown meat on all sides in butter. Pour marinade in skillet and cover. Simmer 1 ½ hours or until tender. Remove meat to warm platter. Add flour and sour cream to skillet. Cook, stirring until thickened. Slice meat and serve with sauce. Serves 6.

Irene Parkinson, West Mifflin

In this recipe, the marinade has a dual role. It tenderizes and flavors the meat, then becomes part of the accompanying sauce.

KARTOFFELPUFFER
POTATO PANCAKES

4 large potatoes	salt and pepper
1 egg	⅓ cup grated onion (optional)
½ tsp. baking powder	
3 tbls. flour	

Wash and peel potatoes. Grate potatoes finely and squeeze out moisture. Mix with all other ingredients. Spoon mix into hot oil in a skillet. Fry until crisp and golden on both sides. Cover and allow pancakes to drain on paper towels. Serves 8.

Traditionally served mit apfelmus (with applesauce). Can also be served with sour cream.

Mary Lou Falce, West Mifflin

DAD'S PORK CHOPS IN SOUR CREAM

1/2 cup flour	1 bay leaf
1 tsp. salt	1 cup sour cream
4 1" thick pork chops	1/8 tsp. thyme
3/4 cup water or chicken broth	1/2 tsp. pepper
2 tbls. vinegar	

Dredge chops with flour, salt, pepper and thyme. Brown slowly. Place in glass casserole dish with cover. In small saucepan, blend rest of ingredients and warm. Pour over chops. Cover tightly, cook at 325° for 45 minutes. Great with mashed potatoes.

Pat Sommers, Munhall

DUMPLINGS WITH SAUERKRAUT

Cook 1 quart sauerkraut adding just enough water to barely cover for 20 minutes.

Mix:

1 1/2 cup flour	1 egg, beaten
1 tsp. baking powder	1/4 cup milk
1/4 tsp. salt	

Cook 5 minutes with cover off and 7 minutes with cover on.

Adele Buck, Penn Hills

BREADED DEER STEAK

1 egg	paprika
parsley flakes	milk
bread crumbs	garlic salt
Parmesan cheese	deer steak

Mix egg, parsley and milk and set aside. Mix bread crumbs, garlic salt, Parmesan cheese and paprika to taste and set aside. Cut partially thawed deer steak in half and when thawed out, dip steak thoroughly in egg mixture, then bread crumb mixture, and fry in hot oil over medium heat until both sides are brown.

Mary Obringer, Whitaker

SAUERBRATEN
BRAISED BEEF

3 lbs. rump roast, boneless
   (all fat removed)
1 ½ tsps. cornstarch
   ½ tsp. margarine

1 lemon, thinly sliced
   pinch sugar
¼ cup low-fat yogurt
   parsley sprigs

Marinade

2 cups Ale
   (dark beer is preferred)
2 cups water
½ lemon
2 bay leaves, crushed
1 onion, sliced

1 clove
1 small tomato, chopped
   few sprigs of parsley
½ tsp. peppercorns
5 cloves, crushed

Mix marinade ingredients and pour over meat. Cover and refrigerate for 2-4 days, turning meat several times. Remove meat from marinade, strain and save liquid. Dry meat and coat with cornstarch. Brown meat in deep frying pan with margarine. Add 1 cup of marinade, lemon and sugar.

Cook covered over low heat on stovetop for 2-½ hours or until meat is tender. Skim fat from sauce. Reheat sauce, add yogurt and blend. Slice meat diagonally across grain, arrange on platter, and spoon sauce over it. Garnish with parsley. Serves 6.

Maria Vamos, West Mifflin

"This is a pared-down version of the popular German dish, Sauerbraten. The heavy cream, butter, bacon fat, and unfortunately, the sausages or "wurst" have been elimi-nated for health reasons. However, our family loves this version and with only 317 calories per serving and 13 gms. of fat, we feel we are still enjoying the taste of Oktoberfest, less the consequences."

BEEF "BARBIE"-QUE

3 lbs. chuck roast (boneless)   1 cup green pepper, diced

6 cups water   1 cup onion, diced

2 cups ketchup   salt and pepper to taste

1 cup celery, diced

Place beef in roasting pan with water. Place remaining ingredients on top. Cover and bake at 350° for 5 hours. All vegetables will be dissolved. Take 2 forks and shred meat. Serve on fresh egg buns. Makes enough for 20 sandwiches.

Barbara Sturms, Duquesne

HAMBURGER SCRAPPLE

2 cups yellow corn meal   1 lb. ground beef

2 cups cold water   1 large onion, finely chopped

6 cups water   1 ½ tsps. poultry seasoning

3 tsps. salt   pepper to taste

Mix together corn meal and cold water and set aside. Bring 6 cups water and 3 tsps. salt to a boil. Lightly brown ground beef, onion and add seasonings. Add the corn meal mixture to the salted boiling water and when it returns to boil, add the meat mixture and simmer covered for 10 minutes. Pour into bread pans that have been rinsed in cold water. Refrigerate until firm. Scrape any fat from top of pan, slice and fry in hot grease browning on both sides. Frying in bacon drippings adds a wonderful taste. Serve with syrup.

Dolores M. Zewe, Duquesne

"Broadside" by Edwin Rowe of Homestead, dated 1892.

NAPF KUCHEN
GERMAN COFFEE CAKE

1 ½ sticks butter or margarine	1 tsp. vanilla
1 ¼ cups sugar	2 tbls. sugar
2 eggs	1 tsp. cinnamon
2 cups flour	chopped nuts
1 tsp. baking powder	raisins
½ tsp. baking soda	powdered sugar
½ pint sour cream	

Preheat oven to 350°. Grease and flour a bundt, angel food or jello mold pan. Mix and cream margarine or butter, sugar, eggs and beat until fluffy. Sift together flour, baking powder and baking soda; add to creamed mixture. Fold in sour cream and vanilla. Pour half the batter in prepared pan. Mix together 2 tbls. sugar, cinnamon, as many chopped nuts and raisins as desired. Sprinkle over batter in pan. Pour remaining batter over all. Bake 45-50 minutes. Let cool 10 minutes before turning out of pan. Sprinkle with powdered sugar.

Dolores Zewe, Duquesne

This recipe has been in the Zewe family for about 60 years.

GRANDMA BUCK'S SOFT GINGER COOKIES

1 cup dark brown sugar, packed	6 ½ cups flour
1 cup lard	4 tsps. baking soda
2 eggs	2 heaping tbls. ground ginger
2 cups dark molasses	1 tsp. salt
1 cup sour milk	1 cup raisins, optional
	1 cup nuts, chopped, optional

Sift or blend well with wire whisk all dry ingredients. Cream brown sugar and lard. Add eggs one at a time, then add molasses and blend well. Alternate dry ingredients with sour cream to this mixture. Stir in raisins and nuts by hand. Drop by heaping teaspoonful onto ungreased cookie sheet and bake 7 minutes on bottom rack and 7 minutes on top rack at 375°.

Kathie Buck, Penn Hills

GERMAN ALMOND COOKIES

1 cup shortening	2 tsps. cinnamon
2 cups light brown sugar	½ tsp. nutmeg
1 cup almonds (cut fine)	1 tsp. soda
1 tsp. vanilla	½ tbls. salt
1 tsp. cloves	3 ½ cups flour

Cream shortening and sugar together; add eggs one at a time. Add almonds and vanilla. Mix spices, salt and soda with flour; add to the creamed mixture and chill overnight. Mold mixture into balls; place on a cookie sheet, then press down with fork. Sprinkle with sugar and bake at 350° for 12 minutes.

BLACK WALNUT CANDY

1 cup cocoa	½ cup milk
1 cup brown sugar	1 walnut-sized scoop of butter
1 cup corn syrup, light	1 cup nuts, chopped

In heavy cast iron skillet, combine all ingredients except butter and nuts. Cook over low heat stirring constantly as this scorches easily. When mixture reaches crack stage, remove from heat and add butter and nuts. Mix until butter melts. Do not beat! Pour into greased pie pans. When completely cool, I put mine in jumbo ziploc bag and crack with hammer. Each piece is individually wrapped in a small piece of wax paper. Our family always doubles this recipe.

Kathie Buck, Penn Hills

Working at the Forge. Photo courtesy Randolph Harris.

SCOTCH-IRISH AND IRISH

The term Scotch-Irish is ancient, initially coined to describe young men attending Scottish universities from the Ulster region of northern Ireland. The compound moniker more generally refers to the Scots who migrated to the northern province of Ireland around 1609. Religious persecution and the ceasing of trade between Ireland and England caused the Scotch-Irish to migrate to America by way of the port of Philadelphia throughout the 18th century.

The Scotch-Irish are best remembered for their determination to pioneer settlements west of the Allegheny Mountains in the early 1700s. They arrived in large numbers after 1725 leaving a trail of churches in their path, preceded only by the Germans.

An enthusiastic people, their ambition was especially acute for the religious fervor of John Calvin. They made Pennsylvania the Presbyterian capital of the country, though there were Scotch-Irish of other denominations. The Scotch-Irish formed a third of the state's population and one-sixth of the colonies' members at the time of the American Revolution, which some feel played a significant part in the battles that ensued. In Stefan Lorant's *Pittsburgh: The Story of An American City*, historian George Bancroft says, "They brought to America no submissive love for England; and their experience and religion alike bade them to meet oppression with prompt resistance. We shall find the first voice publicly raised in America to dissolve all connection with Great Britain came…from the Scotch-Irish Presbyterians."

The excitability of the Scotch-Irish in Western Pennsylvania could also get them into trouble, as the Whiskey Rebellion of 1794 attests. This insurrection ended when George Washington sent in militia to regain civility, but not before federal officers had been tarred and feathered by an irate crowd that refused to pay a new excise tax on whiskey.

The Scotch-Irish Presbyterians have unmistakably molded great portions of Western Pennsylvania, establishing three theological seminaries before the Roman Catholics had any. The founders of many area colleges, such as the University of Pittsburgh and Washington & Jefferson College, the Scotch-Irish were catalysts in politics, education, law, religion, medicine and engineering. Among notable Scotch-Irish Pittsburghers are Stephen C. Foster, Robert Fulton, Samuel Morse and the area's Mellon, Oliver and Jones families.

IRISH CATHOLICS

The siren's song of the "American Dream" played loudly to the thousands of unemployed, hungry Irish in the mid-1800s. By 1850 there were approximately 10,000 Irish immigrants in Pittsburgh, mainly hailing from industrialized Ulster in northern Ireland, and to a lesser degree the counties of Leinster, Munster and Connaught. Comprising the largest portion of Pittsburgh's foreign-born labor force, this wave of immigrants heralded the region's first significant Catholic influx.

Unlike much of the mass immigration from Ireland at this time, Pittsburgh attracted families from the more modernized eastern and central regions where the Great Potato Famine had wrecked less disaster than in the poorer west and south. Yet the desperate need for employment in the new world found 52 percent of the area's Irish workforce in unskilled jobs earning 75 cents a day for back-breaking labor in quarries and dockyards. There was a higher percentage of Irish in this low earning category than any other major ethnic group in 1850. Many families scraped by only because of boarders and child labor.

The Irish in skilled trades often earned their living as iron puddlers, rollers and heaters paid by the ton. Fiercely proud and highly efficient, these Irish Catholics often controlled production, commanding wages of $15 a week. Other ambitious immigrants were peddlers, most visible in Market Square, tailors, shoemakers and blacksmiths.

Though large in number the Irish community lacked cohesion, usually being part of a larger neighborhood and clustering around the local parish. Pittsburgh was a Protestant stronghold into the twentieth century, with anti-Catholic sentiment emerging in the form of arson and cross burnings. This helped keep the Irish entrenched in their neighborhoods and folk culture, further separating them from the changing city. It wasn't until the late nineteenth century that Irish Catholics were able to successfully begin to fight these prejudices and emerge as a force of their own.

"The Ward, 1894" A view of Homestead from the hills that rise above the town. These homes were replaced during WWII with the "Liberty Shops." Courtesy Randolph Harris from the Pennsylvania State Library, Harrisburg

SCOTTISH PANCAKES

1 cup cake flour	1 egg
2 tbls. sugar	2/3 cup buttermilk

Sift flour and sugar together into mixing bowl. Beat the egg until pale yellow, then mix with buttermilk. Pour the egg and buttermilk mixture onto the flour and blend thoroughly. Set aside for at least an hour before cooking. Pour 2 tablespoons batter on hot, lightly oiled frypan or griddle and cook until bubbles appear and begin to break. Turn and cook on other side.

Irene Parkinson, West Mifflin

SCOTTISH EGGS

8 eggs, hard-cooked, peeled,	1/2 tsp. ground sage
at room temperature	1/4 tsp. salt
1/4 cup flour	2 eggs, beaten
1 1/2 lbs. bulk pork sausage	6-8 cups peanut oil
1 cup dry bread crumbs	for deep frying

Coat each hard-cooked egg with flour. Divide the sausage into 8 equal parts. Make a patty out of each bit of sausage, and use it to coat each egg completely. Mix the bread crumbs, sage and salt. Dip the sausage-coated eggs into the beaten eggs; roll in bread-crumb mixture.

Heat the oil to 375° for deep frying. Deep fry the eggs, 4 at a time, 7 minutes minimum. Drain. Serve hot or cold.

Nelli Sigrid Simpson, Crafton

BARLEY AND MUSHROOM CASSEROLE

6 tbls. butter	1 cup pearl barley
2 cloves garlic,	1/2 tbl. dried basil
peeled and minced	3 cups chicken stock
2 yellow onions,	salt and pepper to taste
peeled and minced	1/4 cup chopped parsley
1 lb. mushrooms, thinly sliced	

Preheat oven to 375°.

Melt the butter in a 2-qt. stove-top covered casserole. Add the garlic and onion and saute over moderately low heat until onion is translucent, about 5 minutes.

Add the mushrooms and saute over moderate heat until mushrooms are golden, about 5 minutes.

Add the barley and basil to the mushroom mixture, and toss lightly, then pour in the chicken stock and season to taste with salt and pepper.

Slowly bring the casserole to a boil, then remove it from the heat. Cover the casserole and bake in the oven until the barley is tender, about 45 to 50 minutes.

Before serving, add the chopped parsley and toss gently. Serve hot. Serves 6 to 8.

Nelli Sigrid Simpson, Crafton

SHEPHERD'S PIE

Cook round steak until done in skillet. After it is cooked, put in a baking dish with drippings and layer with sliced onions on top. Cover with thick layer of mashed potatoes. Brush with butter. Heat in oven until hot. Place under broiler until potatoes are browned. Serve with peas.

Marion Lizik, Homestead Park

MINCED PIE

Brown one pound of ground meat and onions. Add carrot strips and cook until tender. Thicken juices and put in lined pie pan. Top crust on pie. Bake at 325° until brown and the crust is done.

Marion Lizik, Homestead Park

SHORTBREAD

2 cups flour	$1/2$ cup sugar
1 tbl. cornstarch, heaping	$1/2$ lb. butter, softened

Place all of the dry ingredients in a mixing bowl and blend well. If you have a heavy-duty electric mixer, cut in the butter with the machine. If not, do it by hand with a pastry blender.

Knead the dough by hand for just a moment and form it into a circle $1/4$" thick on a non-stick baking sheet, and flute the edges. Prick the whole circle with a fork. Bake in a preheated 325° oven for $1/2$ hour, or until it just begins to turn a light golden brown. Allow it to cool for a few minutes, and then remove it to a rack for the final cooling. When cool, the cookie can be cut, but the Scots simply break it up into pieces and serve it with tea. Wonderful!

Nelli Sigrid Simpson, Crafton

SHORT BREAD COOKIES

1 cup butter   2 ½ cups flour

⅝ cup sugar

Use pastry blender (fork) at first to mix dough. Then it is best to use your fingers. It generally takes about one hour to mix. Blend dough until it has the consistency of pie crust. Fingers work best because body heat melts the butter. Shape dough into triangle shape cookies about 1" big. Bake on an ungreased cookie sheet at 300° for 30 minutes or until they are light brown on the bottom. Cook and store in metal tin. These cookies are best when allowed to age one month in a metal tin.

Marion Lizik, Homestead Park

SHORT BREAD CAKE

1 lb. flour   ½ lb. sugar

½ lb. butter

Blend together by hand. Place in round cake pan. Bake at 325° for 30 minutes. If you don't have an oven (as many people in Scotland to this day do not have because of the high utility cost) you may mix ingredients in a cast iron skillet and cook on top of the stove, covered, over low heat for 40 minutes or until light brown.

Marion Lizik, Homestead Park

"Beattie is my ancestry name from the MacBeth and Stuart clans in Scotland. These two old Scottish recipes for Short Bread are from my great-great Aunt Mae Beattie who still lives in Scotland. The Short Bread Cookie style is usually served at Christmas. The Short Bread Cake form was served at high tea."

One can test a cake's baking by drawing it to the edge of the oven and listening for the faint, spattering sound which will continue until it is ready to take out. This is a better trial than the broom splinter thrust into the dough.
Homestead Local News, January 26, 1894

IRISH PROVERB

"Follow steadfast the ways of your ancestors."
The immigrants were poor in arriving, and then became poorer! The menus were
adapted to the foods available in the new world. Meat was costly, potatoes were not.
They did their best and managed to survive to carry on the ways of their ancestors.

OAT BREAD

1 cup rolled oats,	½ cup honey
cooked and cooled	water to mix
dash of salt	2 pats butter, melted
5 cups flour	yeast, dissolved
½ cup molasses	

Thoroughly mix the dry ingredients. Mix in the molasses, honey, butter and some water. Add the yeast and mix thoroughly. Mix into an elastic dough and put into an oiled bowl. Cover and set in a warm place to rise for 2 hours. Knead onto a floured board and form 2 loaves. Put into greased bread pans. Preheat over to 350° and bake about 45 minutes, until golden brown and tested done. Serve warm with butter. Yields 2 loaves.

POTATO BREAD

3 potatoes,	½ cup lard or shortening
peeled and finely diced	2 eggs, beaten
2 cups water	2 tsps. salt
1 package yeast	5 cups flour
4 tbls. sugar	

In salted water, boil potatoes until done, drain and reserve liquid. Let potatoes cool. In the warm reserve, dissolve the yeast. Slowly mix in the potatoes and everything else until of bread dough consistency. Knead until smooth. Place in a bowl, cover and let rise about 3 hours. Punch down dough, flour surface and place into loaf pans. Bake in preheated 350° oven about 25 minutes or until tested done. Yields 2 loaves.

If raised dough is kept several weeks upon the ice, the last baking will be much better
than the first.
Homestead Local News, July 2, 1892

SODA BREAD

1 lb. plain flour	dash of sugar
1 tsp. baking soda	1 cup seedless raisins, optional
dash of salt	2 cups buttermilk

Combine the dry ingredients and thoroughly blend. Add buttermilk and mix to an elastic dough. Knead lightly on a floured board and form a ball. Push out to about 8" round and 2" thick. Put into a greased 8" pan or iron pit with lid on top. Bake about 45 minutes in pre-heated 375° oven until golden brown and tested done. Serve hot with lots of butter. Yield 1- 8" round loaf.

POTATO SOUP

4 potatoes,	dash of flour for thickening
peeled and finely diced	salt and pepper to taste
12 oz. chicken broth	water for volume
1/4 cup butter	(use the potato reserve)
1 onion or scallions, chopped	any garnish,
1 stalk celery, chopped	such as crisp bacon bits
1 can evaporated milk	
or skim milk	

In salted water, boil the potatoes until almost done. Drain and reserve the liquid. Mix in everything else and boil another 20 minutes, adding the reserved liquid depending upon the desired thickness. Serve as is or puree. Garnish. Serves 4.

POTATO CASSEROLE

2 lbs. potatoes,	2 hard boiled eggs,
peeled and diced	peeled and diced
1/4 cup butter	1 small onion, chopped
2 tbls. flour	2 cups milk
	salt and pepper to taste

In salted water, boil potatoes until done and drain. Mix in everything else and mix thoroughly. Put into greased 2 quart casserole and bake at 350° for 30 minutes. Serves 4.

FISH SOUP

3 lbs. whole fish, cleaned	1 cup white wine
2 potatoes, diced	2 pats butter, melted
2 onions, diced	¼ cup flour
2 stalks celery, diced	4 cups of fish stock
sprinkle of parsley	(from the soup pot)
2 pats butter	2 cups cream

In a large soup pot, put the fish, vegetables, parsley, a sprinkle of salt and pepper and water to cover, plus an additional quart of water. Cover, bring to a boil, add butter and wine. Lower heat and simmer for 30 minutes. In another pot, mix the melted butter, flour fish pieces and 4 cups of stock from the soup pot. Bring to a boil, then dump all into the soup pot. Lower heat to lowest, and slowly blend in cream. Simmer another 15 minutes. Serve hot. Serves 4 to 8 bowls. Can be topped with your favorite dumplings.

BACON AND CABBAGE

1 head cabbage, quartered	onions
2 lb. slab of bacon	1 bay leaf
potatoes	salt and pepper to taste

Put everything into a big pot and cover with water. Bring to a boil, lower heat and simmer for 2 hours. Slice bacon and everything else as per serving. Serve hot. Serves 4 to 6.

COLCANNON

1 large potato per person,	1 pat of butter per potato
peeled and diced	salt and pepper to taste
1 head cabbage, chopped	a little milk to mix
1 sweet onion, chopped	any garnish

Boil cabbage and onion in salted water until tender. Boil potatoes in salted water until done. Mash potatoes with butter, salt and pepper and milk until smooth. Gently fold in the cabbage and onion. Mix thoroughly. Top with a good mound of butter and make a design on top and garnish. Can be browned under the broiler in a serving dish. Serves 6.

Traditionally eaten in Ireland at Halloween or All Hallows Day on October 31st, the Vigil of Halloween or All Saint's Day.

IRISH STEW

2 lbs. lamb (neck meat is preferred) cut into bite-size
   pieces
6 potatoes, peeled and cut into
   bite-size pieces
3 onions, thickly sliced

salt and pepper to taste
dash of thyme
dash of parsley
1 bay leaf
water to replace if needed

In a saucepan, layer the meat and vegetables, seasoning the meat layer. Cover with water and bring to a boil. Cover, lower heat and simmer for about 1 hour. Lightly stir and add bay leaf. Cover with water and bring to a boil. Cover, lower heat and simmer for about 1 hour. Serve hot. Serves 6

BOXTY

1 lb. raw potato, grated
1 lb. mashed potato, cold
1 lb. flour
1/4 cup butter, melted

dash of baking soda
salt and pepper to taste
some buttermilk to mix

In a cheesecloth, squeeze the raw potato and catch the liquid in a bowl. Let stand until the starch settles on the bottom. Discard the top liquid. Mix the starch with both potatoes. Mix in everything else. Work into a bread dough and knead until smooth. Roll out 1/2" thick and cut out 3 inch circle cakes. Fry on a greased skillet, both sides, until golden brown. Serve hot with lots of butter. Serves about 6.

Traditionally served on the eve of All Saints Day, All Hallows Eve.

CREAMED BROCCOLI

1/2 lb. (per person) vegetable
2 slices bacon
1 cup milk
   dash of flour (for thickening)

1/4 cup butter, melted
dash of dry mustard
salt and pepper to taste
any garnish

In salted water, boil the vegetable and bacon until vegetable is tender and drain. Combine milk, flour and butter then add to the vegetable. Add remaining ingredients. Stir over low heat until thickened. Serve with any garnish. Optional: Pour a cheese sauce over it. Serves 4 - 6.

GLAZED CARROTS WITH ONIONS

1 lb. carrots,	brown sugar (to thicken)
cut into bite-sized pieces	dash of lemon juice
5 onions, sliced	dash of corn starch
1/4 cup butter	dash of water

In salted water, just enough to cover the vegetables, bring to a boil for 1 minute, reduce heat, cover and simmer until tender. Drain. In another pan, combine the butter and sugar and stir. Add the lemon juice, cornstarch, water and stir. Cook over low heat until thickened. Pour over vegetables, toss and cook until golden brown. Serve warm. Serves 6 to 8.

NEW PEAS WITH FRESH MINT

2 cups new peas	salt and pepper to taste
4 small mint leaves, shredded	dash of water
dash brown sugar	(from the reserve)
3 pats butter	

Place the peas, mint and brown sugar in boiling salted water, cover and boil until the peas are tender. Drain and save a bit of the liquid. Stir in the butter, salt and pepper, and water (if needed). Thoroughly toss. Cover and cook for about 1 more minute over low heat until the liquid steams away. Serve hot. Serves 4 to 6.

The water in which green peas has been boiled should not be thrown away. It has a fine flavor — the very essence of peas. A little stock added, seasoned to taste, makes an economical, delicious wholesome and appetizing soup.
Homestead Local News, December 15, 1893

The bridge, far left, once carried workingmen's traffic to the Structural Mill yards and loading bays. Now it stands a silent vigil over desolate open space.

YELLOWMAN CANDY

16 oz. syrup, any kind	1 lb. brown sugar
1/4 cup butter, melted	1 tsp. baking soda
2 tsp. vinegar, apple or white	1 cup peanuts, optional

Mix the syrup, butter and vinegar then blend in the brown sugar. Stir and form a paste. Boil until a drop hardens in cold water. Remove from heat and stir in the baking soda. Pour onto a greased tin. It will form and harden. Break into fun chunks.

Yellowman is a brittle yellow toffee which has been made by the same family in Ireland for several hundred years. It is usually hammered off from large blocks.

First Federal Savings on Homestead's 8th Avenue as it exists today.

RUSSIANS

In many ways the story of Russian immigration to Pittsburgh is that of most southeastern Europeans, and yet no other major group has been so miscategorized. Often lumped in with Slavs, Lithuanians, Poles and Scandinavians, Russian history literally has become that of others from the region. The Russians the following recipes reflect, are those from Central Russia, what was formerly Southern Russia, and those living between Poland and Russia.

Until the latter quarter of the nineteenth century, 75 percent of Pennsylvania's immigrants were western European, the Irish being the largest group and generally lowest in the caste system. 1882 heralded the "new immigration," the shift of newcomers from northwestern to southeastern Europe, predominately attracting Slavs, Poles and Italians. 1872 marked the first time more than 1,000 Russian immigrants had arrived in the United States in one year, but a decade later the number jumped to just under 17,000. The flood that followed continued to rise until it crested in 1892, when 81,511 Russians entered American ports.

Until 1899 the label Russian was given to anyone who came from what was referred to as the Tsar's government, except Poland, diluting the true impact of these statistics. Once census figures became based on nationality the numbers changed drastically. In 1910 the largest group from what had previously been categorized as Russia, 43.8 percent, were Jews, followed by Poles, 27 percent, with ethnic Russians only totaling 4.4 percent, according to Jerome Davis in *The Russian Immigrant*.

From the earliest days of the twentieth century there was a steady increase in the number of Russians making their homes in the United States, rising to 51,472 in 1913. When World War I began in 1914 the Russian stream dried up, even experiencing reverse immigration as some Russians returned home to fight.

Though the actual number and terminology used for Russian immigrants vary, it is consistently stated the vast majority were very poor, mainly from the lower or peasant classes. Less than six percent arrived on America shores with more than fifty dollars in their pocket. Hence, the immigrants first task was that of his Irish and later Hungarian compatriots, to find work quickly. A new arrival's destination was usually determined by the availability of factory or mine work and the location of an existing Russian community. By 1910 Pennsylvania had drawn almost 25,000 new arrivals for these reasons, a close second to New York. By 1920, 14,000 Russian immigrants had made Pittsburgh their home while nearby New Castle, north of the Steel City, also boasted a thriving Russian community.

SIRNAYA PASKA

2	lbs. farmer's cheese	3	raw egg yolks
1	lb. sweet butter, unsalted	1 ½	cups whipping cream
2	cups sugar	1	cup fruit salad, optional
1	tbl. vanilla	1	cup raisins, golden
1	tbl. almond flavoring	1	cup almonds, toasted

Put cheese through food chopper or sieve twice; set aside. Cream butter and sugar together until almost white in appearance. Add flavorings and beat. Add egg yolks and continue beating. When mixture is thoroughly blended add cheese and mix well. Fold in whipped cream (whipped until firm). Fold in well-drained fruit salad, raisins and nuts. Pour into mold lined with cheese cloth and drain for at least 24 hours in refrigerator. Unmold on serving platter and decorate with dried fruit or toasted slivered almonds. Can also be served with fresh strawberries. This will freeze well.

Martha Ermakov, McKeesport

CTARY NISHKOV STYLE
· BORSCH

Make soup stock from beef, lamb, pork or chicken. Skim. Simmer 1 ½ hours. Saute sauerkraut (preferably homemade) in oil and onions until brown. Add to sauerkraut ½ head sweet chopped cabbage, saute, then add to soup. Add ½ cup tomatoes, 1 can diced red beets and liquid to soup. Add dill, parsley, fresh or dry. Salt and pepper to taste. Simmer for another 20 minutes. Serve with rye bread.

Kitchen of Ksenia Ermakov

HRUTKA

13 eggs

1 qt. milk

3 tsps. salt

$\frac{1}{2}$ cup sugar

1 tsp. vanilla

$\frac{1}{2}$ tsp. nutmeg

$\frac{1}{4}$ lb. butter

Beat all ingredients except one egg and butter with electric mixer. In saucepan, heat these ingredients and butter over medium high heat, stirring constantly, until eggs begin to form curd and separate from liquid. Line strainer with cheesecloth and pout in milk-egg mixture. Tie cheesecloth so that cheese forms ball and suspend it so that it may drip six hours. Remove cloth. Cheese should hold its shape. Beat remaining egg and brush cheese with it. Place cheese in preheated 350° oven 3 to 5 minutes to allow to dry. Slice and serve with peasant bread.

Martha Ermakov, McKeesport

PASKA
PEASANT EASTER BREAD

1 pkg. dry yeast

1 qt. milk, divided

1 cup sugar, divided

$\frac{1}{4}$ lb. butter

4 tsps. salt

4 eggs

12 cups flour

1 cup raisins

Dissolve yeast in $\frac{1}{4}$ cup warm milk to which 1 tsp. sugar has been added. Scald remaining milk and add butter, remaining sugar and salt. Pour into very large mixing bowl and cool to lukewarm. Add yeast mixture and eggs and beat well. Add flour 2 cups at a time, stirring after each addition, until batter is stiff. Add raisins and stir. Scrape dough out on floured board and knead, adding more flour if necessary, until smooth. Place in large, buttered bowl and cover. Let rise until double in bulk, about an hour or more. Punch down and divide into 4 pieces. Separate some dough to use for decoration. Place dough for loaves into 4 greased and floured pans. Form reserved dough into braids, flowers or similar decoration and place on top of rising dough. Let rise another 30 minutes. Bake in preheated 350° oven 1 hour, until golden brown.

Martha Ermakov, McKeesport

PONCHIKI
DOUGHNUTS

1 ¼ cups scalded milk

1 cake compressed yeast, crumbled

¾ cup sugar, divided

4 ⅓ cups sifted flour, divided

⅓ cup butter

1 egg, beaten

1 tsp. salt

salad oil

Cool milk to lukewarm and add yeast and 1 tbl. sugar. Add 1 ½ cups flour. Beat until dough forms. Cover and let rise in warm place about 1 hour. Cream butter and remaining sugar. Add egg and salt and stir into yeast mixture. Add remaining flour. Knead well. Place in greased bowl. Brush with salad oil and cover with towel. Let rise until double in size, about 1 ½ hours. Roll on floured surface to ½" thickness. Cut with a floured doughnut cutter. Let rise until doubled in size, about 1 hour.
Fry in hot oil (370°) until golden brown. Drain on paper towels. Serve hot. Makes about 30 doughnuts.

VEGETABLE BORSCHT

8-10 cups water

2 onions, chopped

1 white potato, peeled and chopped

1 lb. carrots, peeled, whole

10 fresh beets, peeled, whole

1 cabbage, shredded

12 ozs. tomato paste

salt and pepper

1 fresh lemon, juice only

fresh parsley and dill, chopped as garnish

Bring water to boil. Add chopped onions and potatoes, whole carrots and beets. In 10 minutes, remove carrots and beets. Add shredded cabbage. Coarsely grate carrots and beets, then add. Add tomato paste and stir. Add salt and pepper to taste. Bring to a boil, then turn off heat. Add juice of fresh lemon and cover. Serve at any temperature. Garnish with fresh parsley and dill. Can keep in refrigerator up to 1 week. Do not freeze. Keep borscht covered at all times while cooking. Makes 10 servings.

BABA BURGERS

2 medium potatoes	salt and pepper to taste
2 eggs	2 lbs. ground chuck
1 large onion	bread crumbs

Put the first 4 ingredients in blender and blend well. Add to ground meat and mix well. Let sit for 5 minutes. Shape into oval burgers, roll in bread crumbs and brown in oil. Put into a casserole or roaster and bake in oven for 45 minutes at 350°. Can be served plain or with a gravy using 1 cup of mushroom soup diluted with water.

Lydia Yon, Homestead

BEEF STROGANOFF

| 2 lbs. sirloin steak, | 2 onions, chopped |
| cut into 2 x 1/4" strips | 1/2 lb. mushrooms, sliced |

Saute beef and onions. Add a little water at a time. Cook until meat is tender. Add mushrooms, cook about 15 minutes, then add salt and pepper to taste. Add about 2 cups water. Mix 1/4 cup flour with water to make a thickening. Bring meat and water to a boil and add thickening. When thick, put in 1/2 pt. sour cream. Serve over noodles or rice.

Lydia Yon, Homestead

Lydia Yon's grandmother and mother fled Russia to China where Lydia was born. From China she came to Homestead where she has lived for over 40 years.

HERBED LAMB SHOULDER

4 lbs. boned and rolled lamb	1 tsp. thyme
shoulder	1 tsp. marjoram
1 garlic clove	1 bay leaf
2 tbls. fat	salt and pepper
1/2 tsp. ground sage	1/2 cup water
1 tsp. ground rosemary	

Rub lamb with cut garlic clove; brown on all sides in hot fat in heavy kettle; remove meat and pour off fat. Put rack under meat in kettle. Add herbs and sprinkle meat with salt and pepper. Add water; cover and simmer for 3 hours, or until meat is tender. Remove meat and thicken liquid with flour-and-water paste. Salt and pepper to taste. Serves 6.

Martha Ermakov, McKeesport

PIROSHKI

Dough

½ lb. margarine, unsalted and softened	8 oz. sour cream or plain yogurt
3 egg yolks	4-5 cups flour
	1 tsp. baking powder

Savory Filling

1 cabbage, shredded	oil
2 onions, finely chopped	1 egg yolk diluted with
1 lb. carrots, grated	2 tbls. strong tea
salt and pepper to taste	

Dough: Mix margarine, egg yolks and sour cream together. Sift flour and baking powder together and add gradually until dough forms. Roll out on floured surface. Cut into 3" rounds.

Filling: Mix cabbage, onions and carrots together. Saute in a small amount of oil. Add salt and pepper.

Place a teaspoon of filling in center of each pastry circle. Bring edges together and pinch tightly into half moon shapes. Brush with egg yolk diluted with strong tea. Bake at 350° for 15 to 20 minutes or until golden brown. Makes 5 dozen.

SUCKLING PIG
WITH CREAMED HORSERADISH SAUCE

1 suckling pig, about 6 lbs.	½ cup horseradish
10 cups cold water	2 cups sour cream
	salt

Put cleaned and scalded suckling pig in cold water without salt, spices or soup greens. Barely bring to slow boil, then reduce heat immediately. Cover and simmer 1 ½ to 2 hours. The suckling is ready when long-pronged kitchen fork pierces meat easily. Do not over-cook. Let stand 15 minutes after removing from heat. Take suckling up let it drain, place on platter. Let cool, then chill. Mix freshly grated horseradish with sour cream and salt. Add few drops of lemon juice if cream isn't tart enough. Spread over suckling pig, decorate with parsley, and serve.

Martha Ermakov, McKeesport

KOTLETY POD SMETANOL
MEAT PATTIES WITH SOUR CREAM

In a bowl soak ⅔ cup oatmeal in ⅔ cup milk for 5 minutes. Put 1 lb. each of twice-ground beef and pork in a bowl, add 2 eggs, lightly beaten, the oatmeal mixture, ½ cup minced onion sauteed in 2 tbls. butter, 2 tsp. salt, 1 tsp. each of basil and thyme, and ½ tsp. pepper, and blend the mixture well. Divide it into 8 parts and flatten each part into a ½" thick round. Press 1 tsp. chilled butter in the center of each round and push the meat up around the butter to enclose it. Flatten the rounds into patties ½" thick, coat each patty with about 1 tsp. sour cream, and roll it in fresh bread crumbs. In a large skillet cook the patties in 6 to 8 tbls. clarified butter for 4 minutes on each side, or until they are golden brown. Top each patty with 2 tbls. sour cream and simmer the patties, covered for 5 minutes. Garnish the patties with snipped dill. Serves 8.

Martha Ermakov, McKeesport

VARENIKI

Dough

2 cups sifted flour

1 egg yolk

2 tbls. water

Filling

1 cup dry cottage cheese

1 egg

salt and pepper to taste

Dough: Mix together flour, egg yolk and water for form a dough. Knead well. Roll thin on a floured surface. Cut into 4" rounds.

Filling: Mix cottage cheese and egg together. Add salt and pepper to taste.

Place a teaspoon of filling in center of each dough circle. Bring edges of dough together and pinch tightly. Drop into boiling salted water. When done, they will rise to the top. Serve hot with sour cream. Makes 2 dozen.

Always beat sour cream lightly with a fork before adding it to a dish. To avoid curdling, never mix cold sour cream directly into a hot sauce. Cool the sauce somewhat and have the sour cream at room temperature. Stir a bit of sauce into it first, and gradually add that mixture to the sauce.

BLINI
BUCKWHEAT PANCAKES

2 cups flour	2 tbls. dried yeast,
1 tsp. salt	dissolved in
4 tbls. buckwheat flour	1/2 cup warm water

Put in bowl or pot all above ingredients. Add 2 cups water and beat hard. Batter should run off of spoon. Cover with waxed paper and towel. Let rise 1 hour. Fry in oil.

Cottage Cheese Topping

1 lb. creamed cottage cheese	1 egg, beaten

Mix together and put in buttered casserole. Put 3 pats of margarine on top of cheese. Bake at 400° for 45 minutes.

Martha Ermakov, McKeesport

CHEESE BLINTZES
Blintzes

1 cup flour	4 eggs, beaten
1 tsp. salt	1 cup milk

Cheese Filling

1/2 lb. farmers cheese	2 eggs
1/2 lb. dry cottage cheese	1 tbl. sugar
1/2 lb. cream cheese	

Blintzes: Sift flour and salt. Mix eggs with milk. Stir in flour. Mix until smooth to form thin batter. Allow to set for 15 to 30 minutes. Pour only enough batter onto a hot lightly greased 6"-7" skillet to form very thin pancake, tilting pan from side to side to spread batter evenly. Cook on low heat on one side only until top of pancake is dry and browned. Turn out onto clean cloth or wax paper cooked side up. Allow to cool. Repeat until all batter is used.

Filling: Mix all filling ingredients together. Place a tablespoon of filling in center of each blintz. Fold edges over to form envelope. Fry in butter or margarine until brown on all sides or bake in a moderate oven. Serve hot with sour cream or cinnamon and sugar mixture. Makes 10 to 12 servings.

MARINOVANNYE GRIBY
PICKLED MUSHROOMS

1 cup red wine vinegar

2 whole cloves

1/2 cup cold water

5 whole black peppercorns

1/2 bay leaf

2 tsps. salt

2 cloves garlic,
   peeled and crushed

1 lb. small, fresh white mushrooms

1 tbl. vegetable oil

In a 1 1/2 to 2 qt. enameled or stainless steel saucepan, combine the
red wine vinegar, whole cloves, water, peppercorns, bay leaf, salt and
crushed garlic. Bring to a boil over high heat, drop in the mushrooms,
and reduce the heat to low. Simmer uncovered, for 10 minutes, stirring
the mushrooms occasionally, then cool to room temperature.

Remove the garlic from the marinade and pour the entire contents of
the pan into a 1 qt. jar. Slowly pour the vegetable oil on top, secure the
top with plastic wrap, and cover the jar tightly. Marinate the mushrooms in the refrigerator for at least one week.

Serve the pickled mushrooms as a piquant accompaniment to meat
or fish.

Martha Ermakov, McKeesport

RADISH AND EGG SALAD

1 lb. red radishes, cleaned,
   trimmed and sliced

3 eggs, hard boiled,
   peeled and coarsely chopped

1/2 cup sour cream

1 bunch scallions,
   trimmed and chopped

   salt and pepper to taste

2 sprigs fresh dill, chopped

Mix all the ingredients, except the dill, and place in a serving bowl.
Garnish with dill.

TUBE CAKE

1 cup raisins	3 eggs
1 ½ cups boiling water	1 tsp. vanilla
1 ½ tsps. baking soda	3 cups flour
2 cups sugar	½ tsp. salt
1 cup oil	1 cup nuts, chopped

Scald raisins with boiling water. Add soda. Let stand while combining sugar, oil, eggs, vanilla. Beat well. Add raisins and flour mixture alternately. Stir in nuts. Pour into greased and floured tube pan. Bake at 350° for 1 hour or longer, until done.

Dolores M. Zewe, Duquesne

TEA COOKIES

1 cup margarine	2 ¼ cups flour, sifted
½ cup confectioners sugar,	¼ tsp. salt
sifted	¾ cup nuts, finely chopped
1 tsp. vanilla	

Blend first 3 ingredients. Mix flour, salt and ground nuts. Mix thoroughly. Roll into balls and bake until set but not brown in a 400° oven for 10 to 12 minutes. Roll in powdered sugar while still warm and then again when cool. Yields 4 dozen.

Martha Ermakov, McKeesport

KISSEL
RUSSIAN DESSERT

3 cups fruit (strawberries, red	1 cup sugar
grapes, currants, cranberries,	1 tbl. cornstarch,
raspberries, etc.)	for every cup of puree

Put fruit in a pan with just enough water to cover. Bring quickly to a boil. Reduce heat and simmer for 10 minutes. Rub through sieve. Add sugar and cornstarch. Bring once more to boil. Cool to room temperature and refrigerate. Serve cold with cream.

Lydia Yon, Homestead

HUNGARIANS

Hungarians suffered the same inaccurate representation in historical documents as Russians and other eastern Europeans. Their entrance into North America prior to 1900 records their place of origin, but does not differentiate individual's diverse ethnic and cultural backgrounds.

Hungary's borders encircled Hungarians, Slovaks, Poles, Ruthenians, Serbians, Croats, Slovenians, Rumanians, Germans, Vendians, and Gypsies. Religious differences widen the cultural chasms: Roman and Greek Catholics, Greek Orthodox, Protestants, as well as Orthodox and Reformed Jews.

Early Hungarian immigrants left their homelands chiefly due to economic problems. Those that arrived in western Pennsylvania worked for low wages primarily as miners and manufacturers of iron and steel before the turn of the century. The first documentation of Hungarian millworkers was in the early 1880s, though they were noted to have labored in McKeesport mills in vast numbers in the latter part of that decade. The 1892 Homestead Steel Strike spurred a demand for immigrant workers Hungarians quickly filled. Unlike the Irish, who largely resided in typical nuclear families, or the more established Germans, Hungarian laborers arriving before 1900 were usually single, between the ages of 19 and 35 and lived in boarding houses, commonly owned by a fellow Hungarian.

A typical such living arrangement would house 20 to 30 men who slept in shifts. The boarding house served as a naturalization center and substitute family for newcomers, as well as a recruiting center for unscrupulous politicians and a windfall for authority figures who preyed upon immigrants.

While Hungarians eventually rallied around church and their work, it was these two elements of their lives that initially could not get off the ground. Varied denominations created congregations too small to support churches and the individualistic, agrarian backgrounds of many of the immigrants made labor organization a truly foreign concept. The latter was overcome in 1906 with the formation of the Hungarian Workmen's Sick Benefit Federation. This highly influential organization reached a post World War membership of 10,000 and structured Hungarian labor in western Pennsylvania. The Hungarian Catholics organized by 1900, with their first church being built in McKeesport. The Protestants had a harder time getting a foothold.

The economic upheaval of the 1890s shook the hard working community enough to prompt a Protestant minister and several hundred Hungarians to emigrate to the prairies of Saskatchewan to establish an agricultural settlement. The turn of the century saw Hungarians bringing their families over from the "old country" and establishing homes, churches and communities in western Pennsylvania.

The first World War brought a new influx of Hungarians whose way was made easier by the struggles and friendship of their countrymen in this strange new land.

PASKA WITH RAISINS

Place in warm cup and let activate:

1 oz. yeast, crumbled	1 tsp. sugar
1/4 cup warm water	

In large crock bowl, measure then sift:

4 1/2 cups flour

Heat lukewarm in saucepan:

1 cup milk	1/4 tsp. salt
1/4 cup + 1 tbl. sugar	

Beat in 2 egg yolks and a few drops yellow food coloring. Add everything together and knead. Dough is sticky (add more milk if necessary). Cover and place in warm place until doubled in bulk. Turn onto slightly floured table and knead slightly. Cover and let set 15 minutes. Roll into large circle and brush lightly with melted butter. Sprinkle on raisins which have been plumped by boiling water for a few minutes. Roll up like jelly roll. Grease 9" or 10" round pan, 4" high. Place dough in pan and let rise for 1 hour. Brush with egg white and bake on lower rack in oven at 350° for 15 minutes and 300° for 35 minutes. Cover loosely with foil last 10 minutes so that top does not get too dark.

Agnes Markoff, West Mifflin

CREAMED STRING BEAN SOUP WITH KIELBASA

1 lb. fresh green beans	2 medium potatoes, cubed
3 qts. water	3-4 tbls. flour
1 small onion, chopped, optional	1 cup sour cream
	3 tbls. vinegar
1 lb. kielbasa	salt to taste

Cut green beans into 1" lengths. Boil in salted water and onion until almost done. Cut Kielbasa in 3" lengths and cook with cubed potatoes until all are tender. Kielbasa should be cooked at least 20 minutes. Mix flour and sour cream and add to soup. Add vinegar. Bring soup to a boil then shut off.

Agnes Markoff, West Mifflin

Raised by Hungarian immigrant parents, Agnes Markoff submits, by special request, a variety of flavorful Hungarian recipes which she serves with her family's favorite Macedonian-Bulgarian dishes.

HALASZLE
FISHERMAN'S SOUP

1 fresh carp, about 6 lbs., boned and cut into chunks	1 medium green pepper, cut into ¼" rings
1 tsp. salt	1 small hot pepper or a dash of Tabasco sauce
1 medium purple onion, thinly sliced carp head and bones	3 small peeled tomatoes, cored and quartered
1 tbl. paprika	

Put fish chunks in a large kettle and salt them. Set aside. Spread onion slices on bottom of a saucepan large enough to hold the head and bones. Place them on top of the onion and pour on enough water to cover. Sprinkle with paprika and slowly bring to a simmer. Cover partially and simmer for 40 minutes. Strain broth into the kettle containing the fish chunks. Add green pepper rings, hot pepper and tomatoes. Simmer, uncovered, for 15 minutes. Shake pot gently from time to time, but do not stir. Test a piece of fish with a fork — if it flakes, it is done. When done, take kettle from the heat and let stand 5 minutes to settle the soup. Serve hot.

William Penn Association

SAUERKRAUT SOUP

1 large onion	1/2 lb. smoked sausage, sliced
peeled and chopped	salt and pepper to taste
1/4 cup bacon fat or shortening	1 tbl. flour
1 tbls. Hungarian paprika	3 tbls. chopped dill
3 cups sauerkraut, drained	1 cup sour cream
1 garlic clove, crushed	at room temperature.

Saute onion in fat until just tender. Take off stove and stir in paprika. Return to heat and add sauerkraut. Saute, mixing with a fork, for 1 minute. Add garlic and sausage. Season with salt and pepper. Pour in 6 cups water. Cook slowly, covered for 30 minutes. Stir flour and dill into sour cream. Add to soup and cook slowly, stirring, until thickened and smooth. Correct seasoning. Serves 6.

HUNGARIAN GOULASH

1 1/2 lbs. beef, cut into 1" pieces	1 large stalk celery, sliced
1 medium onion, chopped	1 cup canned tomatoes
2 tbls. lard	4 medium potatoes, quartered
1 tsp. paprika	salt and pepper
3 medium carrots, sliced	

Sprinkle 1 tsp. salt and 1/4 tsp. black pepper on beef cubes. Saute chopped onion in lard and add paprika and beef. Let simmer in own juice for 1 hour. Add sliced carrots and celery and 1 cup water and simmer 1/2 hour. Add tomatoes then simmer for another 1/2 hour. Add potatoes and 1 to 2 cups water and simmer until potatoes are tender.

Agnes Markoff, West Mifflin

The Turks introduced paprika, strudel, tomato, and coffee to Hungary.

SZEKELY GULYAS

2 lbs. boneless shoulder pork,
  cut into 1 1/2" cubes
3 tbls. lard or fat
2 medium onions,
  peeled and chopped
1 1/2 tsps. caraway seeds
1 small garlic clove, crushed

2 tbls. Hungarian paprika
  salt and pepper to taste
2 lbs. sauerkraut, drained
1 cup sour cream
  at room temperature
2 tbls. fresh dill, chopped

Wipe pork cubes dry and brown in lard or fat. Push cubes aside and add onions. Saute until tender. Stir in caraway seeds, garlic and paprika and cook 1 minute. Season with salt and pepper. Add enough water to cover ingredients. Cook slowly, covered, for 1 hour. Add more water during cooking, if needed. Add sauerkraut and continue to cook about 30 minutes longer, or until meat is cooked tender. Turn off heat, add sour cream and dill and leave on stove until heated through.

VEAL PORKOLT

2 lbs. boneless veal stew meat
  (or shoulder),
  cut into 1 1/2" cubes
3 tbls. lard or fat
4 large onions
  peeled and sliced

1-2 tbls. Hungarian paprika
  salt and pepper to taste
3 tbls. tomato paste
1 medium green pepper,
  cleaned and sliced

Wipe veal dry and brown in hot fat in a large saucepan or kettle. Push meat aside and add onions. Saute until tender. Add paprika and cook for 1 minute. Add just enough water to cover ingredients. Cook very slowly, covered, for 45 minutes, adding more water if necessary. Add tomato paste and green pepper slices and continue to cook for another 20 minutes, or until meat is tender. It may be necessary to add a little more water, but finished dish should have a thick, rich gravy. Do not stir while cooking, but dish can be shaken now and then. Keep tightly covered throughout cooking. Serve with noodles or dumplings. Serves 4 to 6.

GOULASH WITH SAUERKRAUT

2 lbs. veal or beef, cut in 1 1/2" squares	1 cup chopped canned tomatoes or tomato puree
4 tbls. beef suet or butter	1 cup sour cream
1 1/2 cups sliced onion	2 tsps. paprika
1 clove garlic, chopped	2 tsps. chopped caraway seeds
1 tsp. salt	1 lb. sauerkraut
1/2 tsp. pepper	2-3 tbls. chopped parsley

Saute meat in hot beef fat until lightly browned. Add onions, and cook 5 minutes. Add next 4 ingredients and enough water barely to cover the mixture. Cook slowly until meat is nearly done and the sauce greatly reduced, about 45 minutes. Stir frequently when sauce is cooked down. Add sour cream, paprika and caraway seeds. Simmer 30 minutes longer. Heat sauerkraut. Arrange alternate layers of goulash and sauerkraut in a warmed serving dish. Sprinkle top with parsley. Serves 8.

PAPRIKAS CSIRKE
CHICKEN PAPRIKAS AND DUMPLINGS

1 medium onion, chopped	1 1/2 cups water
4 tbls. lard or margarine	1 cube, chicken bouillon
1 tsp. paprika	2-3 tbls. flour
2 tsps. salt	1 cup sour cream
4-5 lbs. chicken	

Saute onion in fat and add paprika and salt. Cut chicken in parts and brown for 15 minutes. Add water and bouillon cube. Simmer slowly until chicken is tender, then remove chicken. Mix flour and sour cream and add to chicken gravy and bring to a boil. Replace chicken, stir and bring to a boil. Serve with dumplings (nokedli).

Nokedli

2 cups flour	1/2 tsp. salt
2 eggs	1/2 cup water

Combine flour, eggs and salt. Add water. Beat well until dough is gummy. Rinse a flat plate with boiling water. Place dough on plate and cut bite-sized pieces into rapidly boiling water. Boil 2 minutes. Drain and rinse with hot water.

Agnes Markoff, West Mifflin

VEAL GOULASH

2 lbs. veal shoulder	2 tsps. paprika
2 tbls. lard,	1/8 tsp. marjoram
or other shortening	2 cups soup stock
1 large onion, sliced	salt and pepper
2 tbls. flour	4 potatoes, diced

Have veal shoulder cut in 1-2" cubes. Heat lard and brown onion in it. Dredge veal in flour and brown in hot lard. Add seasonings and hot soup stock or water. Cover and cook for 30 minutes. Add potatoes and cook until both veal and potatoes are done, about 30 minutes longer. Thicken liquid with flour smoothed in cold water and serve.

OKORFAROK RAGU
HUNGARIAN OXTAIL RAGOUT

1 carrot, diced	1 tsp. paprika
2 large onions, chopped	1 clove garlic, minced
8 whole peppercorns	1 cup canned tomato puree
1/8 tsp. poultry seasoning	4 1/2 cup diagonally-sliced, pared
2 cups Burgundy wine	carrots
2 oxtails, cut up	1 8 oz. package wide noodles
2 tbls. shortening	2 tbls. butter
3 tbls. flour	2 tbls. poppy seeds
1 tsp. flour	

In a bowl, mix diced carrot, onions, peppercorns, poultry seasoning and wine plus 1 teaspoon salt as a marinade. Add oxtails; refrigerate 3 hours. Remove oxtails from marinade and dry on paper towels. Then in hot shortening, in Dutch oven, brown them well. Stir in flour, paprika, marinade, garlic, tomato puree, 3 cups water and 1 teaspoon salt. Simmer, covered for 2 1/2 hours or until oxtails are fork-tender. Cook, then refrigerate. About 1 hour before serving, skim fat from oxtail mixture, add sliced carrots and simmer covered, for about 40 minutes or until carrots are done. Cook noodles; drain, add butter and seeds. On a heated platter, heap noodles; spoon on oxtail, carrots, some gravy; pass rest of gravy. Serves 6.

William Penn Association

NOODLE-CHEESE CASSEROLE

¼ lb. sliced bacon

8 oz. wide noodles,
    cooked and drained

1 ¼ cups sour cream
    at room temperature

1 cup cottage cheese

⅓ cup minced onion

salt and pepper to taste

Cook bacon until crisp. Drain, reserving 3 tablespoons of fat. Crumble and set aside. Mix reserved fat with cooked noodles, sour cream, cottage cheese and onion. Season with salt and pepper. Spoon into a buttered casserole. Sprinkle with crumbled bacon. Bake in a pre-heated moderate over (350°) for about 30 minutes. Serves 8.

NOODLE GOULASH

4 tbls. shortening

4 lbs. beef, cut in cubes

2 cups minced onion

1 tsp. dry mustard

3 tsps. paprika

2 tbls. salt

½ cup brown sugar

4 tbls. Worcestershire sauce

3 tsps. cider vinegar

1 ½ cups ketchup

4 cups water

¾ cup flour

1 lb. cooked noodles

Melt shortening in pan. Brown meat on all sides and stir in onions. Combine next 4 ingredients. Then combine next 3 ingredients with 3 cups of the water and add to the mustard mixture. Add combined ingredients to meat, blend and cover. Reduce heat and cook for 2 ½ hours or until the meat is tender. Stir occasionally. Blend flour with remaining 1 cup of water and add to meat mixture. Stir until thickened. Serve over cooked noodles. Serves 14 - 16. Ideal for family get-togethers.

PAPRIKA POTATOES

2 medium onions	salt and pepper to taste
peeled and chopped	6 medium potatoes,
2 garlic cloves, crushed	peeled and cubed
3 tbls. lard or fat	1 cup sour cream,
1/4 tsp. caraway seeds	at room temperature
1-2 tbls. Hungarian paprika	

In a saucepan, saute onions and garlic in hot lard until tender. Stir in caraway seeds, paprika, salt and pepper and cook for 1 minute. Add potatoes and enough water to barely cover. Cook slowly, covered, for 20 minutes, or until potatoes are cooked. Stir in sour cream and leave on low heat until hot. Serves 6.

A few crushed caraway seeds enhance the flavor of paprika.

SAVANYU KURMPIL
SOUR POTATOES

3 lbs. potatoes	2 tbls. flour
2 tsps. salt	1/4 cup sour cream
1 bay leaf	white vinegar
1 tbl. butter	dash of fresh ground black
1/4 cup minced onions	pepper

Peel the potatoes and cut into 1/2" dice. Rinse and put in a large pot. Cover with cold water, add the salt and bay leaf, and simmer with the lid on until done, about 25 minutes. Drain and reserve 2 cups of the cooking liquid and discard the bay leaf. Melt the butter and saute the onions until they are soft. Stir in the flour and cook for 2 to 3 minutes. Gradually stir in 1 1/2 cups of potato broth. Simmer for 10 minutes. Add the potatoes and let cool Stir a couple of tablespoons of sauce into the sour cream before adding to the rest. Stir in a few drops of vinegar and grind some black pepper directly over the potatoes. Taste for seasoning, more vinegar may be needed. Reheat just before serving.

William Penn Association

GREEN PEPPER SALAD

4 large green peppers	1 medium onion,
1/4 cup vegetable oil	peeled and minced
2-3 tbls. vinegar	3 tbls. chopped fresh parsley
	salt and pepper to taste

Clean green peppers and cut into strips. Saute in oil until just tender. Remove with a slotted spoon to a small bowl. Strain oil; add with other ingredients to peppers. Chill for 24 hours. Serves 4.

SWEET/SOUR CUCUMBER SALAD

3 large cucumbers,	3 tbls. vinegar
peeled and thinly sliced	1 tsp. sugar
1 medium onion,	1/8 tsp. black pepper
peeled and thinly sliced	1/2 cup cold water
3 tbls. salt	

Sprinkle cucumbers and onions with salt and let stand for 15 minutes. Squeeze out liquid and discard. Mix remaining ingredients and add to cucumbers. Sprinkle with paprika and salt if needed. Chill thoroughly.

Agnes Markoff, West Mifflin

SOUR CREAM SALAD DRESSING

1 cup sour cream	1 tsp. sugar
1/4 cup wine vinegar	salt and white pepper to taste
3 tbls. chopped dill	

Combine ingredients. Chill. Serve with cucumbers, leaving to marinate for about 3 hours, or over lettuce leaves. Makes about 1 cup.

BEETS/HORSERADISH

1 lb. can whole beets	2 tbls. vinegar
1/2 tsp. salt	1 1/2 tsps. grated horseradish
1 1/2 tsps. sugar	

Drain liquid from beets and discard. Grate beets by hand, do not use blender. Mix together all other ingredients. Pour over and mix with beets. Chill thoroughly.

Agnes Markoff, West Mifflin

PALACSINTA
HUNGARIAN CREPES

2 eggs	1 cup water
3 tbls. sugar	2 cups flour
1 tsp. salt	powdered sugar
1 cup milk	

Combine first 5 ingredients and beat well. Add flour slowly and beat to a thin, smooth batter. Let stand at room temperature for 2 hours. Batter may be made up to a day ahead, covered and refrigerated. Return batter to room temperature before using.

Spoon 3 tablespoons batter onto a hot greased griddle, tilting pan to spread very thin. Brown lightly on both sides. Place on heated platter and fill with cottage cheese filling (recipe follows) and roll up. Place in buttered baking dish, sprinkle with powdered sugar and heat in 300° oven until warm through.

Cottage Cheese Filling

1 lb. dry cottage cheese	1/4 cup sugar
1 egg, well beaten	pinch of salt

Combine all ingredients and beat thoroughly.

Agnes Markoff, West Mifflin

DOUBLE DECKER SHEET CAKE

5 cups flour	1/2 lb. margarine
1 cup sugar	2 tsps. shortening
4 tsps. baking powder	1/2 pt. sour cream
2 tsps. baking soda	1 tsp. vanilla
4 egg yolks	

Mix all dry ingredients. Add remaining ingredients and knead. Chill 2 to 3 hours. Divide dough into 3 parts, to be rolled separately. You can patch this dough should it tear. Use pan size 15" x 10".

Roll first part and spread nut filling.

Nut Filling

1/2 lb. nuts, ground	1 tsp. vanilla
1/2 cup light brown sugar	1-2 tsps. milk

Roll second layer and place on nut filling. Spread on fruit filling.

Fruit Filling

2   *cups pie filling (pineapple,*

    berry, strawberry, apricot, or

    preserves)

Roll out 3rd part of dough and cut into strips to make lattice top on fruit filling. Sprinkle on a little ground nuts. Bake 25 to 30 minutes at 350°.

Agnes Markoff, West Mifflin

SZILVAS GOMBOC
PLUM DUMPLINGS

6	*medium potatoes*	3	*eggs*
	salt	8	*tbls. butter,*
18	*purple plums,*		*at room temperature*
	Italian or Hungarian	18	*small sugar cubes*
3	*cups sifted flour*	3/4	*cup dry bread crumbs*

The day before, cook the potatoes in their jackets in salted water. When done, drain. As soon as they are cool enough, peel and force through a ricer. Spread on a cookie sheet and let stand overnight in a cool place to dry. When ready to make the gomboc, pit the plums and set aside. Put the riced potatoes in a mixing bowl (about 3 cups), and mix in the flour and 1 teaspoon salt. Add the eggs, and work the dough together with a wooden spoon and floured hands. Beat in 5 tablespoons butter, a tablespoon at a time and continue to work the dough until it's smooth. Let rise for 20 minutes, then roll out 1/4" thick on a floured board and cut in to 3" squares. To form the dumplings, flour your hands, place a square of dough in your left palm, put a plum in the middle of it and a sugar cube into the pit cavity. Pinch the dumpling closed, and roll it into a round smooth ball. Place it, pinched side us, on a floured board until ready to cook. Just before serving, drop the dumplings into plenty of rapidly boiling water. Do not crowd in the pot. After 1 minute, give the dumplings a stir so they won't stick to the bottom. Cook from 12 to 15 minutes, uncovered, after they rise to the surface. Taste one — the plum should be hot and the dough firm, but not gummy, when done. While boiling the dumplings, quickly brown the bread crumbs in the remaining butter. As the dumplings are ready, lift them out of the water with a slotted spoon, roll them in the browned bread crumbs, keep warm until ready to serve.

William Penn Association

CHEESECAKE SQUARES

2 1/4 cup flour	2 eggs, separated
1 tsp. baking powder	1/2 cup sugar
2 tbls. sugar	2 tbls. flour
1/2 lb. butter or margarine	1/4 cup sour cream
4 egg yolks	2 egg yolks
1 tbl. sour cream	1 1/2 tsp. grated lemon peel
1 egg white	2 egg whites
1 lb. cottage cheese	

Into medium bowl, sift flour, baking powder and sugar. Cut in butter until consistency of cornmeal. Add 1 tbl. sour cream and the 4 egg yolks and work together until dough. Press two-thirds of the dough into a greased 13" x 9" pan in a smooth even layer. Brush with some of the egg white.

Mix the cheese with the 1/2 cup sugar, 2 tbls. flour and 1/4 cup sour cream. Press through a sieve and stir in 2 egg yolks and grated lemon peel. Beat 2 egg whites until stiff but not dry, then fold carefully into cheese mixture. Spread mixture over dough in baking dish in a smooth even layer.

From rest of dough, with palms of hands, roll four pieces into pencil-like sticks, 13" long, one piece 15" long, two pieces 9" long and two more pieces 5" long.

Now lay the four 13" sticks lengthwise on the cheese filling. Next, lay the 15" stick diagonally across the center top, from one corner of pan to the other. Then lay a 9" stick diagonally on either side of the 15" one, 2" apart. Lastly, in same way, lay the two 5" sticks, one to the left and the other to the right of the 9" stick. Brush sticks lightly with rest of egg white, then bake cheese cake 7 minutes in a 400° oven. Then reduce oven heat to 375° and bake cake 40 minutes longer, or until golden.

Let cool in pan on wire rack until lukewarm, then cut into squares, sprinkle with confectioners sugar and serve ... or serve cold.

Ann Hrivnak

An old postcard depicting turn of the century Pittsburgh with a vista of the steel mill in Hazelwood, downriver a few miles on the opposite river bank from Homestead. Note the old Pittsburgh Post Office and the glass works.

Part of the legacy left by Andrew Carnegie is the Homestead branch of the Carnegie Library, actually located in Munhall. This photo shows the state of the building undergoing renovations for the 1992 celebration of the events in 1892.

MOLASSES
CARRYING MOLASSES IN BULK

Almost all the molasses which comes from Cuba to the United States is brought in the same tanks in steamships that are used to carry petroleum as a return cargo. The ships' tanks are about sixteen feet deep and have a neck seven feet deep. They are pumped full of oil at Brooklyn or Philadelphia, then taken to Havana, and the oil is pumped out into the tanks of the refining plants there. Molasses is brought from the interior of the island in huge hogsheads which are emptied into the storage tanks. A suction pump drawing about 10,000 gallons an hour fills each ship's tanks to within about two feet of the top, that amount of space being required for the expansion of the molasses. It might be supposed that the petroleum would have a bad effect on the molasses, but it has been shown that the contrary is the case, and as nearly one-half the importation is made into rum and the balance refined into sugar, a little oil is not of much account. The tanks are cleaned after the molasses has been pumped out by turning in a powerful steam jet, which washes down the sides and liquifies whatever molasses may be left in the bottom of the tank, and the suction pump finishes the work.

A cargo of molasses, which formerly required ten or twelve days, can now be unloaded in forty-eight hours, while the difference in the cost of handling, to say nothing of the saving of time, amounts to a large sum.

Homestead Local News, January 19, 1894

MOLASSES CAKE

½ cup sugar	1 tsp. ginger
1 cup molasses	1 tsp. cinnamon
1 tbl. lard, heaping	1 tsp. vanilla
2 cups flour	½ cup warm water

This cake should be baked in a sheet 1" - 2" thick. When baked, ice with 1 cup powdered sugar moistened with 2 ½ tbls. boiling water, flavored with vanilla. Cut in squares when served.

The Daily Messenger, July 9, 1918

SOFT MOLASSES COOKIES

1 ¼ cups sugar	2 ¼ tsps. salt
2 ¼ cups molasses	4 tsps. ginger
2 ¼ cups shortening	2 tsps. cinnamon
1 ⅛ cups buttermilk	6 cups flour
3 ⅓ tsps. baking soda	

Heat molasses, melt shortening in it, cool and add sugar. Mix again. Add buttermilk and then the flour which has been sifted with the dry ingredients. Let stand in refrigerator overnight. Roll about ⅓" thick. Sprinkle with sugar before cutting. Bake in moderate oven at 350°.

GINGER SNAPS

½ cup sugar	1 ½ tbls. ginger
1 cup molasses	1 tsp. cinnamon
1 tsp. soda, heaping	salt
1 egg, not beaten	1 tsp. vanilla
⅔ cup lard, not melted	flour

Mix as soft as possible and bake in a quick oven.

The Daily Messenger, July 9, 1918

CARAMELS

Mix 1 cup of molasses, 1 cup of brown sugar and two tbls. butter. Boil until a spoonful dropped into cold water forms a soft ball between the fingers. Add 1 cup chocolate, cook 3 minutes, and turn into well-buttered pans. Add nut meats if desired. Cut into squares with a buttered knife when nearly cold.

Pittsburgh Press, January 15, 1917

WORLD WAR I

Pittsburgh was a spectator in the Great War for much less time than the rest of the country. As one of the nation's preeminent industrial centers, the Steel City began producing munitions by December 30, 1914 for what was then seen as a European problem. By the time the U.S. joined the war three years later, munitions from Westinghouse plants and steel from area mills were blanketing Europe, mainly contracted by Great Britain, Russia, France and Italy.

The war boosted the Pennsylvania economy and offered a plethora of jobs, but there were fewer and fewer workers to fill them as 60,000 Allegheny County men went off to fight. Immigration was cut to two-thirds at the onset of the Balkan conflict, another cause of the labor shortage faced by the 124 area manufacturing plants built in 1916. The answer, according to Dennis Dickerson in *Out of This Crucible*, was recruiting 18,000 southern blacks in two years to operate the waiting machines.

Pittsburgh "became known as the arsenal of the world," says Frank Murdock in *Some Aspects of Pittsburgh's Industrial Contributions to the War*. "In it were located 250 great war plants, employing more than 500,000 men and women, constantly engaged day and night, in many instances seven days a week, turning out war supplies for the United States and its Allies."

While 3.5 million shells and 80 percent of the U.S. Army's steel came from Pittsburgh, the city also contributed innovative gas mask, optical glass, and munitions forging technology to the war. Unparalleled idea development and production rates — the Carnegie Steel Company set a world's record by producing 100,000 shells in one month — helped make the area's war tonnage five to ten times as great as any other similar sized industrial center in the world, according to Murdock. Many of the products produced by Pittsburgh companies were not something the manufacturers had made before, yet they were often produced in less time and greater quantity than asked.

War-related contracts totalling 215 million dollars were given to Pittsburgh by the U.S. Government in World War I, with one company alone, Westinghouse Electric and Manufacturing, taking in $1.5 billion.

HOW TO COOK GAME

A great many housekeepers are chary about cooking game, as though there were some mystery in it proper preparation, and a good deal of nonsense has been talked about "rare" game which has perplexed and warned off the ordinary person, who has no appetite for raw flesh. As a rule, all dark-fleshed birds, like ducks and grouse, should be cooked about as rare as roast beef, so that the blood runs from the knife. Birds with white flesh, like partridge, should be as well done as a barnyard fowl. A simple rule for time allows eighteen or twenty minutes roasting for either canvas back or redhead duck, fifteen minutes for teal, eighteen or twenty minutes for grouse, twelve or fifteen minutes for doe-birds, ten minutes for either plover or woodcock and eight or ten minutes for English snipe. Tender, plump quail requires from fifteen to eighteen minutes, and the average plump partridge from thirty-five to forty minutes. This implies the briskest heat the range oven can give, a heat that will turn a sheet of writing paper dark brown in ten minutes.

Homestead Local News, December 22, 1893

SPINACH CROQUETS

With the contents of a can of spinach mix 2 tbls. of butter, 1 tbl. of minced parsley, 1 tbl. of sugar, grated rind of 1 lemon, salt and pepper to season. Add a half cup of milk, heat thoroughly and cool. When cold shape into croquets, dip in egg and crumbs and fry in deep fat.

Pittsburgh Press, January 13, 1917

AN ECONOMICAL DINNER

Take a good-sized pie dish, put in a layer of sliced potatoes, then a layer of sliced onions, shake over a few lentils, then add a little rice. Repeat these layers until the dish is full. Put a few small pieces of dripping on the top, and season with pepper and salt. Pour in sufficient water to moisten the vegetables, cover with suet crust, and bake in a moderate oven for 2 hours. This is a cheap, wholesome and very tasty dinner.

Gazette Times, June 4, 1915

WHEN IS A CUP NOT A CUP?

Before the war you knew how to cook. You knew what should be the consistency of a pancake batter or a cake dough. In all cases you had you own recipes, good old "stand bys" treasured in the family for generations gathered from cousins, friends and neighbors, or made up out of your own head under the stress of circumstance.

But war conditions have made many of your recipes impractical. Wheat flour no longer figures in the recipes of the one hundred percent patriotic. And calls have gone out for recipes which use the new flours.

They include barley flour, oatmeal, oat flour, corn flour, cornmeal, rice flour and buckwheat.

In the experimental kitchen of the United States Food Administration certain general things about these wheat substitutes have been found to be true. Seemingly they will not substitute in a recipe "cup for cup" and give good results. But "weight for weight" the results are excellent. Women this bit of news would seem , if we were English or Canadian, very practical. In those countries they do most of their cooking with a pair of scales instead of a measuring cup. But we American women have never done that, and so for the present at least, we should like a translation into measuring cups.

Fortunately this has been arranged. The following table will show you how much of each of the common substitutes to use in place of a cup of wheat flour — both the bread flour and the pastry flour.

In place of a cup of wheat flour (bread flour) use:

1 ½ cups barley flour	⅞ cup (generous) coarse cornmeal
1 ⅓ cups ground rolled oats	
1 cup corn flour	⅞ cup (generous) rice flour
1 cup (scant) fine cornmeal	⅞ cup (generous) buckwheat
1 cup (scant) oat flour	

In place of a cup of wheat flour (pastry flour) use:

1 ⅓ cups barley flour	⅞ cup (scant) oat flour
1 cup ground rolled oats	¾ cup coarse cornmeal
⅛ cup corn flour	¾ cup rice flour
⅞ cup (scant) fine cornmeal	¾ cup buckwheat

In most recipes except those which use yeast as a lightening agent, these substitute very nicely for wheat flour. Even in yeast breads a very high proportion of them can be used.

The Daily Messenger, July 6, 1918

SEED BREAD

Required - Four ounces of butter, two pounds of flour, half an ounce of caraway seeds, a quarter of an ounce of spice, half a pound of moist sugar, one pint of milk, one ounce of yeast, and one teaspoonful of castor sugar.

Rub the butter into the flour, add the seeds, also the spice and sugar. Mix all well. Warm the milk and cream together and the spice and sugar. Mix all well. When this is liquid, strain it into the tepid milk. Pour into the middle of the flour. Make the mixture into a light dough and knead it well. Line a cake tin with greased paper. Put in the dough, and place the tin in a warm place until the dough rises to twice the original size. It will take about an hour. Then bake in a moderate oven for two hours.

Pittsburgh Gazette Times, June 4, 1915

BROWN POTATO SOUP

A savory, nourishing, meatless soup is quickly prepared from a half-dozen potatoes, pared and cut into dice; a couple of blades of celery cut small and a half onion chopped fine, all cooked in salted water until tender. Place in the skillet a tablespoonful of butter, heat and stir in about three tablespoonfuls of dry flour, a pinch of salt and a little pepper. Keep rubbing and stirring the flour until evenly browned over a slow fire. While the soup is boiling and bubbling sift in the brown flour, stirring the soup all the while to prevent the flour from lumping.

Pittsburgh Press, January 15, 1917

OYSTER SANDWICHES

Scald half a pint of oysters in their own liquor until the edges curl. Then drain and chop coarsely and add a tablespoon of lemon juice, salt, pepper and a tiny pinch of cayenne. Spread between slices of buttered whole wheat bread.

Pittsburgh Press, January 15, 1917

ROAST GOOSE WITH GOOSEBERRY SAUCE

Select a goose with a clean, white skin, plump breast and yellow feet. Prepare and truss in the usual way, stuffing it with a good onion and sage stuffing. Roast the bird from for 1 - 2 hours, according to the size. The giblets may be stewed, then chopped and added to the gravy, or be made into a little pie. Serve the goose as soon as it is cooked, so that it does not flatten at the breast before sending to the table. Garnish with fresh cress and parsnip fritters. Serve with gooseberry sauce.

Pittsburgh Press, January 13, 1917

HOTCH-POTCH PIE

Take a deep pie dish and place in it a layer of slices of cold cooked veal, and then a layer of cooked potatoes, cut into slices. Next some slices of ham, then a layer of hard-boiled eggs, and so on until the dish is full. Cover the top with potatoes cut into slices. Pour a teacupful of good gravy into the pie, and take for three-quarters of an hour in a moderate oven. Scatter seasoning between each layer of meat. Serve hot.

Pittsburgh Gazette Times, June 4, 1915

ESCALLOPED PEACHES

Cover the bottom of a buttered baking dish with cracker crumbs. Add a layer of canned peaches, season with bits of butter, a little cinnamon and a tablespoon of sugar. Add a second layer of crumbs, peaches and seasonings.and an upper layer of buttered crumbs. Bake 45 minutes and serve with a vanilla sauce.

Pittsburgh Press, January 13, 1917

GINGER APPLES

Use equal quantities of apples and sugar. Firm, green apples are best. Pare, core and quarter them and put them into cold water. Put the sugar in a kettle and to every pound of it add half a pint of water and bring to a boil. Add the apples and one-half pound whole ginger, dried. Boil until the apples are clear and can be pierced with a straw. Put in jars and seal in the usual way. Serve with cup custard.

Pittsburgh Press, January 15, 1917

COOKIES

One cup butter, two cups sugar, a small teacup sweet milk, half a grated nutmeg and five cups of sifted flour, into which has been sifted two teaspoonfuls of baking powder; mix into a soft dough and cut into round cakes. The dough should be rolled as thin as pie crust. Bake in a quick oven to a light brown. When water is substituted for the milk the cookies will keep longer. These cookies can be made with sour milk if a teaspoonful of soda is dissolved in it, or sour or sweet cream may be used in place of butter.

Pittsburgh Press, January 13, 1917

Wash six ounces of rice, add to it two quarts of boiling water, and three ounces of raisins, boil very gently for half an hour, then strain. This will be found a capital drink to give children when there is any indication of diarrhea.
Pittsburgh Courier, 1911

SHORT PASTRY

Use one-half pound of self-raising flour, one-quarter pound of lard and butter, one-half teaspoonful of salt, water to mix.

Rub the butter and lard into the flour, to which add the salt. Mix to a stiff paste, and roll it out on a floured board. This pastry is excellent for fruit tarts, pies and dumplings.

Pittsburgh Gazette Times, June 4, 1915

BUTTER SCOTCH

This is the easiest of all candies to make. Mix one pound of sugar with three tablespoons of water and melt in a porcelain saucepan. Add three tablespoons of butter and simmer without stirring until a spoonful tested in cold water becomes brittle. Turn into well buttered pans and set aside to cool. Cut into squares with a buttered knife before the candy hardens.

Pittsburgh Press, January 15, 1917

People cultivate nerves to a large extent, and do not apply simple rules to cure them.
Healthy work, particularly out of doors, is an excellent antidote to nerves.
Onions are a very good tonic for nervous people.
Cranberries are good for sufferers from inactive livers.
Pittsburgh Courier, 1912

The east entrance to Open Hearth No. 4 and the Structural Mill yards that used to lie beyond the railroad tracks.

AFRICAN-AMERICANS

Southern blacks' general dislike of organized labor made them attractive as strike breaking recruits to Pittsburgh industry as early as 1875. "The presence of non-union blacks convinced white employees that mill owners deliberately tried to use blacks 'to put down the white labor.' In some instances, these sentiments led them to retaliate violently against blacks who ignored the strikes and remained loyal to local iron and steel officials," wrote Dennis Dickerson in *Out of This Crucible: Black Steelworkers in Western Pennsylvania, 1875-1980.*

They may have been given jobs, but little pay for their effort. In 1907 blacks fell into the 12-19.99 category of wages established by Margaret Byington. This allotted approximately 24 cents a day per man for meals. Most black workers resided in boarding houses.

The Great Migration between 1916 and the 1930s heralded the largest influx of African-Americans to Pittsburgh, mainly from Virginia, Georgia, Alabama and the Carolinas. The two decades between 1910 and 1930 saw the Steel City's black population increase 115 percent to 55,000 with the number of black steelworkers increasing 626 percent in the same period.

The great steel strike of 1919 and demands on the city from the Great War provided blacks an opportunity to negotiate for better wages. Unfortunately their good fortune was often fleeting, frequently being the first ones laid off in times of depression.

It wasn't until the Wagner Act in 1935, giving workers the right to collective bargaining, that blacks were allowed to join unions. Still, discrimination for black workers lingered longer than other ethnic groups and at the destruction of Lower Homestead in 1941 many black millworkers were told they were not eligible for the government housing provided for the displaced families.

The colossal labor demands of the second World War encouraged 10,500 more blacks to put down roots in the Steel City, leading to a 6.5 percent population in the 1950 labor force.

A TALE IN BLACK AND WHITE

John he askin duh boy his name
and from wha he done run away
telling John he done come a mighty fur piece up duh road
and down home dey calls 'em Joebey
say he been brung up hea in a quaker man's
wagon bottom covered all up wid hay
say he been hidein hea since day for yestaday
been eatin vittles he been carryin all duh way from
duh Souf in a poke (bag) stuffed down in dat
slave picked cotton blouse
wid his feets feelin dat blessed northern grown
his mouf feeling like it wanna shout
duh quaker man sayin "hush up an stay down
somebuddy be hea to fetch yo out"
but yo bes keep inside dees graveyad bouns
dem pattyrollers huntin runaways wid dey niggah
eating houns
den John askin Joebey what he got in his mine ta do?
say he ain't come up wid no answea (answer)
an say he been goin ovea duh same thang too
he jus standin dere lookin
din his eyes lighten up like sunshine
John askin 'em what he knows bout cookin?
Joebey say he meetin up wid a ol' man call
Jeremiah, when dey boff done run away
sayin, he done showed 'em bout cookin duh vittles
we done stole at night
an we hidein out by day

say he laughin fit to kill when Jeremiah tole 'em
dem critters outa duh barnyad field or book
see a niggah comein wid a pot or pan
day knows dey goose is cooked
Joebey saying don't know what y'all does bout eatin
up hea in duh north
but a darky take up a pan done dar in duh Souf
dey comes up wid vittles dat make dees soldiers
layin in dis graveyad raise up an smack dey moufs
duh way deys fryin chicken hits fitten fo God above
when dey cooks fo a gatherin of duh folks in duh
quarters day be doin hit outa luv
he sayin when Jeremiah makes kush
dats cone bread cooked ona duh open fire
big slab ub dat bread smeared wid butta
ain't no finea eatin wid a bowl ub jambalaya
Roxanna be fryin up a mess a fish on a saturday
nigh dippin hit in duh meal den trawin hit in
duh hot grease in duh pan
folks be sittin roun till eatin time
Samuel he be pickin duh banjo Keeba she be movein
duh heat roun wid a turkey feathea fan
duh mens roun duh lasses barrel shufflin cards
roun playin coon can

---

*Excerpts from "A Tale In Black And White" an epic book length
poem about slavery written in dialect by Vera B. Hubbard.*

AFRICAN-AMERICANS

Africans, brought to America in bondage and used as slaves, were put to toil in the fields of many white land owners. While working in the fields, many slaves identified the wild greens growing as those that were comparable to the greens from their native country. They picked the greens and dried them over an open fire all day long while they worked the fields. To the greens they added hamhocks which were discarded from the "main house" for flavoring. During slavery, what the whites rejected, blacks ate. What is now known as 'soul food' today is descended from dishes made by slaves making do with their masters' livestock castoffs: pigs' feet, hindparts, jowls, intestines, cow brains and tongues, among them. Slaves made the best of the situation and turned a source of humiliation into a cultural celebration. When all the preferred vegetables were taken, the slaves cooked the bitter collard, mustard and turnip greens in pork leftovers. The food slaves ate was informally called "make-do". After the Civil War many impoverished whites found that emancipated slaves chose to stay on to serve and work among white Southerners. In this climate, "make-do" food began its transformation to Southern food and is accepted today in many white, as well as black, households.

COLLARD GREENS

1 *large hamhock*	3-4 *tbls. bacon grease*
1/4 *lb. saltpork*	1 *tbl. chicken bouillon*
1 *medium onion, diced*	3 *lbs. collard greens*
2 *tsp. sugar*	

Place first 6 ingredients in a large pot with enough water to cover. Heat thoroughly and bring to a boil. While water is heating, wash greens. If greens are particularly dirty, use a small amount of dishwashing liquid and rinse thoroughly, 3 or 4 times, with clear cold water. Remove stems, roll up the greens, and cut into small pieces. You may use a variety of greens (i.e., kale, turnip or mustard greens) and mix a pound of each together. Place the greens into the pot after 30 minutes. Cook an additional hour or until greens are tender and you are able to get a fork through the hamhock. Additional water may be added throughout the cooking process if greens begin to stick. Cook down until broth is almost gone. Before serving, remove hamhock, dice and add to cooked greens. Excellent served with warm buttered cornbread.

Hattie Thoms, West Mifflin

SHRIMP PILAU

4 thick slices bacon	1 tsp. salt
1 1/2 cups chopped onion	2 cups rice
4 ripe red tomatoes, peeled, seeded and chopped	3 cups Shrimp Stock, below (use heads and shells of shrimp called for here)
1/2 tsp. hot red pepper flakes, or to taste	1 1/2 lbs. shrimp, or bodies from 2 lbs.
3 tbls. chopped parsley, plus some for garnish	heads-on shrimp, peeled

In Dutch oven with a tight-fitting lid, cook bacon on top of stove until crisp. Remove bacon, set aside to drain, and pour off all grease except about 3 tbls., or enough to cover bottom of pan. Add onion and cook over medium-low heat for 5 to 10 minutes, until transparent. Add tomatoes, red pepper flakes and parsley and cook for another 5 minutes. Add salt, rice and stock, raise heat for a moment or two, and bring to a simmer. Lower heat again, cover pot and simmer for 20 minutes without raising lid.

After 20 minutes, lift lid and fluff rice with big fork while tossing in shrimp. Cover pot and turn off heat. Pilau will be ready in 5 to 10 minutes and shrimp will not over-cook. Crumble reserved bacon and garnish pilau with it and some parsley. Serve with a tossed salad and corn bread. Makes 4 to 6 servings.

Shrimp Stock

2 lbs. fresh heads-on shrimp	handful of fresh herbs such as thyme, parsley, basil, oregano and savory
3 qts. water	
1 large carrot	
2 celery ribs	1 medium onion, quartered but unpeeled

Remove heads and shells from shrimp, dropping heads and shells into an enameled or stainless steel stockpot. Cover shrimp bodies with plastic wrap and store in refrigerator to use later.

Add rest of ingredients to stockpot and cook, uncovered, at a low boil until onions are transparent and the stock is pleasantly infused with shrimp flavor — about 45 minutes. Liquid will be reduced to 2 qts. Strain out the solids. Cool, then freeze what you don't plan to use immediately.

CORNBREAD

3 cups self-rising cornmeal	16 oz. sour cream
4 eggs	16 oz. creamed style corn
1 cup oil	1 tsp. sugar

Mix all ingredients thoroughly. Pour into greased or sprayed pan. You may use a round or square pan. Bake at 350° - 375° for 25 to 30 minutes until bread is lightly browned on top. Cool slightly so it will cut easily. Serve warm with butter or margarine.

Hattie Thoms, West Mifflin

SWEET POTATO CASSEROLE

3 large sweet potatoes	4 tbls. butter
1 tsp. salt	8 marshmallows
1 tsp. cinnamon	1/3 cup chopped nuts
1/2 cup crushed pineapple,	
well drained	

Boil sweet potatoes until tender, peel and mash. Brown the butter and add to potatoes. Add remaining ingredients, mixing after each. Put in greased baking dish and bake 35 minutes in moderate oven at 350°. Place 4 marshmallows on top, return to oven and brown lightly.

AFRICAN CHICKEN

3 lbs. boneless, skinless	3 cups water
chicken breasts	2 1/2 tbls. ketchup
2 large onions, chopped	3/4 cup peanut butter
2 tomatoes, chopped	1/4 tsp. cayenne
2 cloves garlic, crushed	3 hard boiled eggs, sliced
1 tsp. salt	

Place first 5 ingredients and 2 cups of the water in a large saucepan. Bring to a boil. Reduce heat, cover and simmer for about 30 minutes.

Stir in ketchup. Mix together the peanut butter and remaining cup of water. Add to chicken, cover and simmer for 1 hour.

Add cayenne and eggs and serve immediately.

Irene Parkinson, West Mifflin

SHRIMP CREOLE

1/4 cup green pepper, cut into strips	1/3 cup water
1 medium clove garlic, minced	2 tsps. lemon juice
1 tbl. butter or margarine	dash Tabasco sauce
1 can condensed tomato soup (10 3/4 oz.)	1 lb. cooked shrimp
	2 cups cooked rice

In saucepan, cook green pepper with garlic in butter until tender. Add remaining ingredients except rice. Heat, stirring occasionally. Serve over rice. Makes 4 to 6 servings.

SWEET POTATO PONE

4 large sweet potatoes	1 cup milk
1/2 orange rind only, grated	1/2 cup butter
1 lemon rind only, grated	1/2 tsp. cinnamon
2 eggs beaten	1/2 tsp. nutmeg
1/2 cup brown sugar	1/2 tsp. cloves
1/2 cup dark molasses	

Grate raw potatoes and orange and lemon peel. Mix beaten eggs and sugar. Add sweet potatoes, grated orange and lemon peel, molasses, milk, butter and spices. Pour mixture into greased baking dish and bake slowly (325°) for 50 to 60 minutes. Serve hot or cold. Serves 8.

Vera Hubbard, Verona

OLD FASHIONED HOECAKE

1 cup corn meal	2 tbls. bacon fat
1 cup flour	water
1/2 tsp. salt	fat for frying

Combine dry ingredients adding enough water to form a soft batter. Melt bacon fat in black iron skillet and fry hoecake. Brown slowly. Turn and brown other side.

Vera Hubbard, Verona

This batter was cooked on a hoe held over a fire in the fields at meal time by the slaves thus named "hoecake".

SCALLOPED PINEAPPLE

2 ½ cups sugar

1 ½ sticks butter

3 eggs

9 slices white bread, cubed

¼ cup milk

1 20 oz. can crushed pineapple

Cream the sugar and butter together. Add the eggs and set aside. In a separate bowl, pour the milk over the cubed bread. Mix in the pineapple including the juice. Take your creamed mixture and add it to the bread mixture, stirring thoroughly. Bake at 350° for one hour in an ungreased casserole dish. Serve hot as a dessert topped with whipped cream. May also be served as a side dish to any meal.

Hattie Thoms, West Mifflin

SWEET POTATO PIE

2 ½ lbs. sweet potatoes

½ cup sugar

½ tsp. nutmeg

⅛ tsp. cinnamon

1 tsp. vanilla

¼ cup butter

2 eggs beaten

¼ cup evaporated milk

1 unbaked 9" pie shell

Boil sweet potatoes in skins until tender. Drain, peel and mash well. Blend in sugar, nutmeg, cinnamon, vanilla and butter. Fold in eggs. Add evaporated milk and beat mixture until fluffy. This makes a generous amount of filling. Flute sides of pie shell high to hold it. Leftover filling can be baked in small baking cups, if desired. Pour into pie shell and bake in 300° oven for 35 to 40 minutes or until lightly browned. Serves 8.

Vera Hubbard, Verona

UKRAINIANS

Pennsylvania was the destination for almost fifty percent of the Ukrainian tidal wave that hit the Atlantic coast between 1877 and 1930. Though using inexact ethnic records, Ukrainians, or Ruthenians as they were often categorized, came to the Keystone State largely from the provinces of Ruthenia and eastern Galicia, which fell under the Austro-Hungarian empire until 1918.

Mass migration was spurred by economic depression, a state that had left half the Ukrainian immigrants to America illiterate. Long persecuted by their Polish and Hungarian neighbors, the Ukrainians were ripe recruits for a Pennsylvania coal company seeking mine laborers to break a long strike. Though these early immigrants were received with much hostility by older immigrants who saw them only as strike-breakers, the money they sent home started a major exodus from the Ukraine.

The years before World War I saw Ukrainians settled throughout the state, especially in Pittsburgh, Homestead, McKeesport, McKees Rocks, Butler, New Castle and Johnstown. By 1934 the region boasted 115 Ukrainian organizations, with most immigrants working as manual laborers in factories and mines. The wages were low, averaging 30 to 32 cents an hour for common laborers, 48 to 60 cents for skilled mechanics.

The dissection of the Ukraine after World War I sent more Ukrainians to American doorsteps, where many of their countrymen had learned to read and write and become citizens. A few individuals headed away from the factories to become farmers in Erie County while others established small businesses in immigrant communities like the South Side.

Pittsburgh was the Ukrainian center of the region, with numerous ethnic publications, hundreds of fraternal societies, and ten Ukrainian churches in the city. Though Ukrainians spent a long time living in below standard conditions, often waiting years to send for their families, they became recognized as civic-minded and cooperative, though historian Wasyl Halich asserts they like to argue politics and religion among themselves.

UKRAINIANS

CHICKEN KIEV WITH MUSHROOM SAUCE

4 chicken breasts,	¼ lb. butter,
boned, halved and pounded	chilled and cut into 8 sticks
to form cutlets	2 eggs, well beaten
1 tbl. chopped green onions	fine dry bread crumbs
1 tbl. chopped parsley	

Sprinkle salt, onions and parsley over cutlets. Place a butter stick at one end of cutlet and roll in jelly roll fashion, tucking ends inside. Roll in flour. Then dip in well beaten eggs and fine dry bread crumbs. Chill for 1 hour. Fry chicken rolls in deep fat for 5 minutes or until golden brown. Serve with mushroom sauce (slightly diluted cream of mushroom soup) and lemon wedges.

Millicent Bibza Skarzynski

When drawn butter separates or decomposes from standing too long, add a tablespoonful of cold water or a small lump of ice and beat until is becomes smooth.
Homestead Local News, December 15, 1893

UKRAINIAN NUT TORTE

12 egg yolks	1 lb. nuts (walnuts or pecans),
½ tbl. vanilla	ground
2 ½ cups powdered sugar	12 egg whites
	1 tbl. fine bread crumbs

Beat egg yolks and vanilla until thick. Gradually add sugar and beat well until thick. Stir in the ground nuts. Fold in beaten egg whites alternately with bread crumbs. Bake at 320° for 1 hour.

Icing

2 whole eggs	1 egg yolk

Beat well together and add:

6 tbls. sugar	½ lb. unsalted butter
8 tbls. strong coffee	

Combine whole eggs and egg yolk and beat well together. Add sugar and coffee. Put in double-boiler and stir until it thickens. Water should be hot, but not boiling. Do not overcook or it will curdle. Cool. Add butter and beat until creamy and smooth. Spread between layers and on top.

SOUR CREAM COOKIES

½ cup butter	1 tbls. lemon extract
1 ½ cups sugar	3 cups all purpose flour, sifted
2 eggs	1 tsp. baking soda
1 cup sour cream	½ tsp. salt

Cream together butter and sugar. Add eggs, sour cream and lemon extract. Sift together flour, baking soda, salt and add to cream mixture. Drop by tablespoonful on dry cookie sheets and bake at 375° for about 10 minutes. Do not turn. Makes 3 dozen.

UKRAINIAN APPLE SQUARES

3 cups flour, sifted	1 cup sugar
1 tbl. sugar	4 tbls. flour
1 tsp. salt	1 lemon, rind only
1 cup butter or margarine	2 tsps. cinnamon
2 egg yolks	1 cup nuts,
5 tbls. milk	finely chopped
3 lbs. apples	½ cup sugar

Sift together flour, sugar, salt; cut in butter or margarine as for pie crust dough, add egg yolk and milk. Toss together and pat into a ball. Put in refrigerator for about an hour. In the meantime, slice apples and add sugar, 4 tbls. flour, lemon rind and cinnamon. Combine all ingredients thoroughly. Take ⅔ of dough and roll out and place in 9" x 13" pan. Put apple mixture over the dough. Roll out the rest of the dough and cut in 1 inch strips and criss-cross over the top. Mix nuts and ½ cup sugar. Sprinkle over top. Bake in 350° oven for 1 hour.

Water color painting of a Ukrainian kitchen from pre-revolutionary Kiev, circa 1912. Artist unknown. Courtesy Dan Karaczun.

Russian immigrant family, 1921. Courtesy Dan Karaczun.

THE DEPRESSION YEARS

Charity rears its unhappy head even now when the golden bounty of summer lies all around us. Rich fields are yielding their ripened grains, succulent vegetables come from gardens and orchards offer their colorful, fragrant offerings — yet to many they must pass unheeded. The depression is not over for everyone. Some have seriously reduced incomes that mean scanty menus. Still others must depend on welfare agencies for their daily food.

Tons of flour and thousands of cases of evaporated milk are now being distributed to these unfortunates. We must help them to convert these two mainstays of the diet into nourishing appetizing dishes. Many homemakers must struggle along with lack of information and without the aid of practical suggestions. To meet the situation, companies and organizations have worked our recipes to guide such families.

Plenty of milk and bread supplemented with the cheapest leafy vegetables like cabbage, spinach and field greens with oranges or tomatoes several times a week will furnish a diet that will maintain the health of the individuals as well as appetizing low cost dishes on the economy menu. Canned milk should be mixed with an equal quantity of water for drinking and served either hot or cold, plain or with a dash of cinnamon, nutmeg or salt.

CANNED MILK FOR BAKING

Use canned milk freely in baked foods for the fine flavor and the food value that it adds. Here is a recipe for a light-bread that is good and is easy to make.

Crumble two cakes of compressed yeast into a bowl, add two tablespoons sugar and one-third cup barely warm water. When soft add three cups of liquid (diluted canned milk, half and half), four teaspoons salt and two tablespoons melted fat. Add ten cups flour all at once and work in thoroughly with the hands.

When the dough is well mixed, knead it gently in the bowl until smooth, round it up, put in a warm place to rise. When the bread has doubled in bulk, knead the dough and let rise again. Divide the dough into four portions and let stand, covered for fifteen minutes then shape into loaves and put into greased pan. Let rise for an hour then bake in a hot oven fifteen minutes. Reduce the heat and continue baking for thirty to forty minutes. This makes four loaves.

The Daily Messenger, September 8, 1933

COTTAGE PUDDING

For cottage pudding, cream two tablespoons of fat with one cup of sugar until light, then add an egg and beat well. Add one-half teaspoon vanilla extract. Sift together two cups of flour one-half teaspoon salt and four teaspoons baking powder and add alternately with one cup of diluted milk to the creamed mixture. Bake in a square layer cake pan in a moderate oven. Serve warm or cold with the following sauce:

Mix one cup of sugar, two and one-half tablespoons flour, a pinch of salt and a few gratings of nutmeg. Add one cup of boiling water and cook until clear., stirring constantly. Add one cup of evaporated milk and continue cooking until well blended and slightly thick. Remove from the fire and add two teaspoons of butter and two teaspoons of vanilla. This will make six to eight generous servings.

The Daily Messenger, September 8, 1933

World War I Memorial in Munhall Park which lies between The Carnegie Library of Homestead and St. Michael's R.C. Church.

STUFFED TOMATO SALAD

2 large firm tomatoes	1/2 tsp. salt
1 egg, hard-boiled	dash of paprika
1/2 green pepper, chopped	2 tbls. mayonnaise
1 tsp. chopped onion	1/2 cake cream cheese
1/2 small cucumber, chopped	

To be added when ready to serve:

4 tbls. mayonnaise	lettuce and watercress

Serving four.

Dip the tomatoes in boiling water for a minute, then plunge them into ice water, so the skins will peel off readily. Hollow out the centers and place the tomatoes in the icebox to chill while the stuffing is prepared. Chop the egg very fine and add seasoning, green pepper, cucumber and onion. Mix with mayonnaise.

Work the cream cheese and beat with a fork until it is light and creamy. Spread a thin layer of cheese inside each tomato shell, then carefully put in the egg filling, taking care not to scrape the cheese lining from the shell. Chill for several hours until very firm then cut each tomato into four slices. Just before serving arrange on beds of lettuce and watercress and add one tablespoon mayonnaise to each serving.

The Messenger, May 27, 1930

COCOANUT MOUSSE

1 egg white, unbeaten	few drops of almond extract
1 cup heavy cream	1/4 tsp. vanilla
1/2 cup sugar	1 cup cocoanut, toasted and
pinch of salt	cooled

Combine egg white and cream in a small bowl and beat with a rotary egg beater until stiff. Add sugar gradually, beating well. Add salt, flavoring and cocoanut. Pour into a mold, cover with waxed paper. Pack in equal parts of ice and salt, and let stand for 6 hours, or until firm. This recipe makes one and one half pints of mousse. This can be served as it is, or it is delicious with a fruit sauce.

The Messenger, May 20, 1930

You have to be dead twenty-five years to get in the Hall of Fame, which makes quite a few Senators eligible now.
The Messenger, May 20, 1930

Joseph Palyo family, 1916. Joe worked as a Heater in the Structural Mill soaking pits and lived with his family in the Ward. Courtesy Joanne Siket Karaczun.

MACEDONIANS

Some historians credit Macedonians with suffering the greatest hardships of any European peoples. Five centuries of harsh oppression under the Turks forcibly initiated the tradition of Macedonians migrating to other lands, especially to neighboring Balkan countries. Struggling for recognition of their country, the land once called Macedonia stretches through northern Greece, Bulgaria and former eastern Yugoslavia. Until the 1992 war in Yugoslavia, Macedonia was recognized as one of that country's independent republics, creating a unique renaissance for its people.

"Emigrating in large numbers, they adapted themselves to the customs and conditions and learned the language of the cities in which they established their home. A hard-working and intelligent people, the Macedonians did not lose their identity but soon began to make their mark on the social, political and cultural life of the country where they settled," says Giorgio Nurigiani in *The Macedonian Genius Through the Centuries.*

Approximately 200,000 Macedonians migrated to North America by World War II. Those that settled in western Pennsylvania united with the Bulgarian community, initially being paid poor wages for millwork. A small but active community of 100 families today, Bulgarian-Macedonian families totaled 500 at their strongest.

The Bulgarian-Macedonian Club, established in 1935, is frequently identified as the community's unifying force. Founded by a Macedonian, the organization would put on plays and have dances, and sometimes a wrestling match. The association was designed to look out for the community, especially in times of need. When nine members died in 1962, threatening to exhaust their funds, it was determined no one else could die for three years. No one did.

While there are larger Macedonian-Bulgarian enclaves in Los Angeles, Detroit and Toronto, Pittsburgh's community has remained active. Starting out as steel workers and shop owners facing discrimination, area Macedonians have become educators and community and civic leaders — taking great pride in their dance performance at the yearly Folk Festival.

INTERVIEW
Nicholas and Agnes Markoff, West Mifflin

Lambe and Nevena Markoff arrived in West Homestead from what is now Yugoslavia in 1905. They built a small oven in the basement of their West Eighth Street apartment, and the West Homestead Baking Company was created.

Baking 20 loaves daily, Lambe would take the bread to Hazelwood by trolley, where he sold them door-to-door. As business grew, he acquired a horse-drawn wagon, and in 1906 moved the company's location to a larger space next door.

In 1924 Lambe built and moved his family into a three-floor apartment on the corner of West Eighth and Forest Avenues in West Homestead. The first floor was occupied by a confectionery store and a barber shop that was later converted to a butcher shop. Lambe, his wife and their six children occupied the second floor.

In 1929 the building also housed the newly-formed Bulgarian-Macedonian Beneficial Association (BMBA), which Lambe founded and served as its president. Three years later the association received its charter, and in 1935 built the Bulgarian-Macedonian Club on West Eighth Avenue in West Homestead.

By the 1940s the West Homestead Baking Company had grown to 20 routes, trucks, drivers and 15 "bobtailers" (independent contractors). Their noted specialty: sour dough round rye bread, 25-cents a loaf.

A fire in 1958 destroyed the business. It was later reopened, but insurance didn't cover the costs of full restoration, and business fell off. "We patched up but business started going down," recalls Lambe's son, Nick. "A&P was charging $1 for three loaves of bread."

Lambe's grandson, Edward Markoff, is president of the Bulgarian-Macedonian Club, which remains active in the Steel Valley, despite having less than 100 members.

MACEDONIAN STUFFED CABBAGE WITH EGG AND LEMON

1	head of cabbage	water
3	lbs. ground beef	3 eggs
1 ½	cup rice	½ lemon, juice only
	onion powder to taste	½ cup water
3	cubes of beef bouillon	

To blanch cabbage leaves, core cabbage and insert large meat fork in center. Place head in boiling water in dutch oven for a few seconds until leaves can be easily removed. Remove all leaves that will be large enough to stuff. Brown ground meat and add rice. Season with onion powder to taste. Roll filling in cabbage leaves. Place rolls in a 4 quart dutch oven. Cover with bouillon dissolved in water. Place a plate on top of the cabbage rolls to stop them from floating. Cook 1 hour on low heat. Be careful that not all the water is absorbed. Add boiling water as needed. When cabbage is cooked, remove any liquid and place it in a saucepan. Meanwhile, separately beat the eggs, ½ cup water and lemon juice until smooth. Pour the reserved broth into the egg-lemon mixture and beat well. Heat, stirring constantly with a wooden spoon. Spoon onto individual servings.

Mary Hodges

ELIA'S STEW

2 lbs. boneless chuck roast, cut into 2" pieces	4 cloves garlic, diced & chopped
water	parsley flakes
4 onions	paprika
4 hot peppers, diced	1 can tomato soup
	ketchup

Cover meat pieces with water and simmer until tender on low heat (do not overcook). Remove foam from top as it forms. In separate pot fry the onions and cleaned out hot peppers in oil to cover. Add a little butter to this also. Take garlic cloves, add a little salt and fry with onion mixture. Add parsley flakes and paprika to color when onions are translucent. Add tomato soup. Meat should be tender and ready. With slotted spoon take meat and add to onion mixture and let meat and onion sauce get acquainted. Strain broth from beef and add to mixture. Better if on thick side, so add little dobble of ketchup. Let it get acquainted more. You have a delicious hot meal. Serve with your favorite buttered bread.

Evie Stoyanoff

EASY MLECHNIK
TRUE MACEDONIAN CHEESE PIE

9 eggs	1 ½ cups warm water
8 oz. softened cream cheese	¾ cup of corn oil
1 lb. Greek feta cheese	1 box filo (defrosted)
2 cups warm milk	

Preheat oven to 350°. Beat eggs for 10 minutes. Add softened cream cheese, milk, water, corn oil and mix together. Crumble and add feta cheese. Overlap 2 sheets of filo crosswise on pan, just as you would use tissue in a gift box. Dip remaining sheets 2 at a time in egg mixture, grab some feta from the bottom of the bowl and place in pan. Fill pan with filo dipped in egg mixture and feta in this manner. When pan is full, fold the overlap of filo on top of the pan, pour remaining mixture on top, making sure all filo is moist. Bake in a 9" x 13" glass pan for approximately 1 hour, until golden brown. Let sit for ½ hour before you cut Mlechnik.

Evie Stoyanoff

BULGARIANS

Bulgaria was one of the last European nations to send immigrants to America, starting around 1905 and continuing through World War II. Poor knowledge of English and a dearth of marketable skills led Bulgarians to follow the growth of industry, stopping in places with mill, mine or railroad work and then moving on when they were no longer needed. The first Bulgarians in western Pennsylvania, mainly young, single men living in boarding houses, worked predominately in the mills, but like others from their homeland, many did not expect to remain in the United States. In fact, the number of Bulgarians who returned to their country between 1910 and 1929 eclipses the number that stayed.

Often changing, but continually oppressive, governments caused many Bulgarians to flee their country, with the largest influx reaching Pittsburgh between 1912 and 1913, the height of the Balkan War. The majority came to the Steel City from the Bulgarian capital, Sofia, in the west, with a few hailing from the central region, known for its magnificent roses.

They settled around the mills, in West Homestead, Homestead, West Mifflin and Clairton. At its zenith the Bulgarian-Macedonian community encompassed 500 families, which has dwindled to about 100 today. Their homeland split among Bulgaria, Greece and former Yugoslavia, Pittsburgh Macedonians identified closely with the Bulgarian community.

Bulgarians exhibited a strong pride in their culture, an emphasis on education, and a gift for hospitality, making those that didn't work in the mills good entrepreneurs. At one time, according to Clarke Thomas in *They Came to Pittsburgh...*, 33 Pittsburgh bakeries were run by Bulgarians, with one in Homestead operated as a partnership between 17 Bulgarians and Macedonians.

Most Bulgarians attended Russian Orthodox Churches, especially St. Gregory's in Homestead, as there is no Bulgarian Orthodox church in Pittsburgh. Other members of the community have gravitated more towards the Greek Orthodox or Roman Catholic churches.

They may not have had their own church but they did have the Bulgarian-Macedonian Beneficial Association as of 1935, an influential organization that allowed no politics on their agenda, even from displaced Bulgarians who had fled communism in World War II.

Bulgarian's emphasis on learning and preserving their traditions has earned wide recognition for their small community, which plays a key role in the area's annual Folk Festival.

Slovak immigrants, circa 1910.
Courtesy Joanne Siket Karaczun.

INTERVIEW
Diana Jordanoff Kaye, West Mifflin

Born in Bulgaria in 1901, Diana Jordanoff Kaye came to
Pittsburgh in 1920 after marrying a Bulgarian railroad worker who
had been in America for 15 years. The couple started a grocery
store on 7th Avenue in Homestead, but lost their business in 1939
when an A&P market opened in their area.

"Everything was welfare in those days," recalls Diana.
"People would cash their checks and go to the A&P where prices
were lower, and when they ran out of money they would come to
our store and buy on credit. We lost our business because we had
no cash to buy our goods. I went around to collect some money and
people would pretend they didn't know me and would close their
doors."

World War II and a resultant labor shortage came, and
Homestead Steel began to hire women. Diana was one of the first
women hired in the mill — at $6.48 a day — "a lot of money in
those days." Her husband desperately pleaded with her not to go
to work at the mill. "He was ashamed that our people would see
me doing that kind of work."

Diana was put to work in Carrie Furnace, pushing wheelbar-
rows and loading bricks onto railroad cars. She was transferred
three months later to "the best job I ever had" in the mill's machine
shop. She worked there until the end of the war, when she was laid
off due to both the drop in the demand for steel and the returning
men who were given their jobs back. After her $21-a-week unem-
ployment checks ran out, she worked as a seamstress at
Carlynton's Men Shop in Homestead until 1952.

With money Diana and her husband had saved from his job
at Mesta and her job with U.S. Steel, they bought shares in the West
Homestead Baking Company and they both worked there. "They
made the best rye bread! There were 32 Bulgarian bakeries in
Allegheny County at that time. Ours was the biggest plant.

Diana obtained her first refrigerator in America at May-Stern in Homestead. Because they could not afford to buy one, a refrigerator was installed in their home that contained a meter box. Each time they wanted to use the appliance, they put coins in a meter and the electricity would go on until the metered time ran out. An employee from the store would periodically come to the house and empty the coin box. The appliance was not officially Diana's until the cost of the unit was collected from the meter box.

While working in the mill her typical lunch was a salad made of green peppers, vinegar, oil and garlic, and a sandwich, either cheese, egg or meat. White dry beans were the main dish of all Bulgarians, says Diana. "If you had nothing else to cook, you always had a pot of beans on the stove. Now you can't even buy beans, they're so expensive."

POPSKA YAHNIA
VEAL AND ONION STEW

2 lbs. veal, cubed	1/4 tsp. pepper
water	1 tbl. parsley
2 tbls. tomato paste	3 tbls. flour
2 tsps. salt	2 bags frozen small onions

Saute meat. Add water to cover meat. Blend in tomato paste and seasonings. Simmer slowly for 60-75 minutes. Thicken with flour dissolved in cold water. Bring back to boil. Add thawed and drained onions. Bring back to boil and simmer for 1/2 hour.

Diana Jordanoff Kaye, West Mifflin

YOGURT

1/2 gallon milk	1/2 cup yogurt starter
	or plain yogurt

Bring milk to a boil and allow to cool until small finger can be inserted in the milk for the count of ten. Add cooled milk to starter, 1 tbl. at a time, until the starter is the same temperature as milk. Pour diluted starter into the remaining milk. The milk can then be placed in a casserole or individual containers. Place container(s) in a bowl or wrap with newspaper and place in oven with the pilot light on for 4 to 5 hours. Remove, chill and enjoy.

Diana Jordanoff Kaye, West Mifflin

Cheese can be made from the yogurt by wrapping it in three layers of cheesecloth, tying it in a "sack" and hanging from your sink faucet until the whey has dripped out to make the yogurt cream cheese consistency. Tangy and delicious! Add onions if you like.

TARATOR
COLD CUCUMBER SOUP

3 cups yogurt

½ cup water

1 large cucumber, chopped fine

1 clove garlic

1 tbl. vinegar

salt and pepper to taste

Mix yogurt and water until consistency of buttermilk, then add rest of ingredients and serve as a cold soup.

Diana Jordanoff Kaye, West Mifflin

FASUL OR BOP
WHITE BEAN SOUP

1 lb. white beans (Great Northern)

½ cup olive oil

2 onions, finely chopped

2 qts. water

½ cup canned tomatoes

1 garlic bud

salt and pepper to taste

paprika

mint (optional)

Soak beans in saucepan for five hours. Drain, rinse and cover with cold water. Bring to a boil and add other ingredients. Continue to boil for about 1 hour or until beans are done. Season to taste. Serves 5 to 6.

Patricia Jordanoff French, West Mifflin

YAGNI, SPINAK I ORIS
LAMB, SPINACH AND RICE

2 lbs. lamb, cubed

2 tbls. margarine

3 tsps. salt

¼ tsps. pepper

2 tbls. parsley

2 packs frozen leaf spinach

1 cup long grain rice

2 tbls. tomato paste

water

Brown meat in margarine. Add water to cover meat. Blend in tomato paste and seasonings. Simmer on low heat for 1 hour. Add frozen spinach to meat and bring back to boil. Add rice and cook for ½ hour. Check for water and seasonings.

Diana Jordanoff Kaye, West Mifflin

KORABEEKI
YOGURT COOKIE

1/3 lb. lard, melted	1 tsp. salt
1/4 lb. margarine, melted	1 heaping tbl. baking soda
1 1/2 cups yogurt	1 heaping tbl. baking powder
2 1/2 cups sugar	1 heaping tsp. baking powder
7 eggs, keeping 2 whites separate	8 cups flour
	1 cup nuts, chopped
1/4 cup corn oil	1/4 cup sugar

Melt lard and margarine together. In large bowl, put yogurt, sugar, eggs slightly beaten, melted lard, margarine, oil, salt, first heaping spoon of baking powder and soda and mix well until fluffy. Add flour and second spoon of baking powder and mix well. Put 4 cups of flour on dough board, add dough from bowl and knead it on part of flour until dough is soft. Roll out little at a time until dough is 1/4" thick. Cut with cookie cutter. Top with mixture of sugar and nuts. Beat 2 remaining egg whites until stiff. With spoon put a little stiff egg whites on center of cookie, then dip in nuts and sugar mixture. Bake on cookie sheet, greased with corn oil, at 350° for 8 to 10 minutes or until golden brown.

Diana Jordanoff Kaye, West Mifflin

APPLE STRUDEL

Filling

3/4 cup sugar	4 large Rome apples
1 tsp. cinnamon	banitza dough
1 large cup nuts, ground	(recipe follows)

Sprinkle stretched dough with oil. Mix together the sugar, cinnamon and nuts. Sprinkle this mixture onto three-fourths of dough. Peel, grate and squeeze the apples and sprinkle on top of sugar mixture. Trim edges of dough and lay on top of sugared areas. Make sure to oil these pieces. Roll up the strudel with help of cloth as a nut roll. Cut into three strips and lay on a large cookie sheet. Bake at 375° about 45 minutes, until brown.

Patricia Jordanoff French, West Mifflin

BANITZA
FLAKY STRUDEL DOUGH

5 cups flour	2 tbls. melted lard
1 tsp. salt	2 cups lukewarm water

To make dough: Put flour and salt in large bowl. Make well in center. Put melted lard into well, work up to soft dough with warm water. Place dough on a floured surface and knead for 15 to 20 minutes until smooth and elastic. Cut into two pieces, knead again to make smooth balls. Put the two smooth balls on a greased pan and grease well all over with melted lard. Cover with wax paper and let dough relax for 45 minutes to one hour in a warm place. Cover kitchen table with a clean cloth. On a separate floured area roll out one dough as much as you can with a rolling pin. Reach under the dough to its center and lift slightly, being careful not to tear. To stretch, gently but firmly pull it out with the tips of your hands. Do not lift all around. Try not to tear dough, but if this should happen do not try to repair it. Keep pulling and stretching dough, draping it over edge of table. Continue until dough is paper thin. Remove all heavy edges as this will spoil finished pastry. Allow stretched dough to dry 5-10 minutes until a few dry spots begin to appear on dough sheet. This will depend on the warmth of your kitchen. Continue from this point with filling recipe.

Cottage Cheese Filling

4 eggs, slightly beaten	4 tsps. margarine, melted
3 cups cottage cheese	1 1/2 tsps. salt

Spinach Filling

4 eggs, slightly beaten	1 onion, chopped
2 cups cottage cheese	4 tsps. margarine, melted
1 cup chopped spinach	1 1/2 tsps. salt

Fry onion and spinach until soft and add to other ingredients.

Leek and Cheese Filling

4 eggs, slightly beaten	6 leeks, chopped
1 lb. cottage cheese	4 tsps. margarine, melted
1 onion, chopped	

Fry onion and leeks until softened and add to other ingredients.

To assemble banitza: Using banitza dough, place 4 layers of dough on pan, fluff each and fit into pan spreading melted butter between each layer. Put ⅓ of filling on top of 4th layer. Place 4 more layers of dough in pan spreading melted butter on each layer. Put ⅓ of filling on top of 8th layer. Place 4 more layers of dough in pan spreading with butter, then ⅓ of filling and lastly 4 more layers of dough. Bake in 350° oven for 15 to 20 minutes or until golden brown. You may also use phyllo leaves in place of banitza dough.

Patricia Jordanoff French, West Mifflin

Detail of cover photo of a Slovak immigrant. Courtesy James Getsy.

SLOVAKS

Like the Ukrainians, the Slovaks came to American shores in search of something better than the oppressive lives they endured under Austro-Hungarian rule. The majority arrived during the Industrial Revolution of the late nineteenth century and continued to migrate through the 1950s. By 1907, 51.7 percent of Pittsburgh steel workers were Slovaks, mainly living in the city's 2nd Ward in Lower Homestead.

Initially considered socially "inadequate" for their peasant-like lifestyle and lack of schooling, the Slovaks were among the lowest wage-earners in the mills. To compensate, many families took in boarders — 43 percent in 1907. Most of the homes were two room tenements, forcing families to wrestle with the burden of extra people in insufficient space — often generating more hardship than the boarder's contributions offset.

The "Hunkies" — a not so affectionate moniker for immigrant millworkers from Austro-Hungary — faced some of the most difficult steelmaking tasks. "Their labor is the heaviest and roughest in the mill, handling steel billets and bars, loading trains, working in cinder pits; labor that demands mostly strength but demands that in large measure," says Margaret Byington, in *Homestead, the Households of a Mill Town*.

Food was a crucial part of Slovak life. In 1907 Slovak families spent 45.7 percent of their earnings on food, higher than any other ethnic group. Though this is in part because they received lower wages, Slovaks would opt to live in poor housing to have extra money for edibles. The menu was the kind of filling foods that stick to the ribs — meals of bread and meat being the most common. Slovak women generally chose foods easy to prepare rather than the least expensive because of their monumental work load between family, boarders and home, explaining the absence of tedious to prepare vegetables.

As the group settled into their new country they were recognized as hard working, reliable, patriotic and honest.

The Slovak life was festive, weddings and holidays being memorable events. Most were Roman Catholic, establishing numerous churches, and social, cultural and religious organizations. A smaller number were Slovaks of Orthodox beliefs, tied more to Moscow than Rome, owing to their being mistaken as Russians by Americans. Area Russian Orthodox priests are often of Slovak descent.

Saint Michael's parish in Munhall. One of the Slovak Catholic Churches in the valley. This parish is noted for having sponsored the Slovak participation in the Pittsburgh Folk Festival for many years with its excellent food booth, display, chorus and dance group.

INTERVIEW

Straka's, Homestead

Julie Tarasevich's great-grandparents came to Pennsylvania from Czechoslovakia at the turn-of-the-century. When her great-grandfather was killed in a mining accident near Wilkes-Barre, her great-grandmother returned to the home country with their children.

Her grandfather — three years old when his father was killed — was discontent in Czechoslovakia and returned to the United States at age 17, and wound up in Homestead working in the mills. He married, and while he labored in the mills his wife ran a Slovak confectionery store in lower Homestead.

Her grandparents started a kitchen in the confectionery store when her grandfather tired of the unsteady mill work, and in 1925 Straka's Bar was born. "At that time you could make money by accident in Homestead. Anything that was managed properly would make money," said Julie.

Straka's — serving Homestead for the past 67 years — was a favorite haunt for decades of millworkers who would go there to cash their checks, bend elbows with their mill brothers, and feast on Straka's famous roast beef sandwiches.

They were also one of the Second Ward businesses forced to relocate for the mill expansion required during World War Two. *(See section on World War II history.)*

"When America went to war, U.S. Steel needed more room to expand for the war effort, and the property [on lower Ann Street] was seized," said Julie, manager of Straka's. "For a year my grandparents couldn't move anywhere or build anything because of war rationing. They had to rent a home in Squirrel Hill for 10 months." The young couple later built Straka's at its present location on Ann Street.

When prohibition was repealed in 1937, Julie's grandfather "had a friend" who worked for the Liquor Control Board who helped him get the second liquor license issued in Allegheny County, she recalled. The same "friend"also tipped them off during World War II that whiskey was going to be rationed. "My grandfather went to the liquor store with $5,000 and said 'I want all the whiskey you can sell me for this amount. I don't care what

brand it is.' So when rationing came and they looked at everyone's quota, my grandfather had the highest in Homestead," said Julie.

When the mills first started closing in the late 1970s, "We didn't feel it that much at first," said Julie. "People still came to Homestead and shopped here." But later "business really dropped off. I mean, it really dropped."

The future of Straka's in contingent on an economic recuperation in Homestead, said Julie. "I'd like to say we're going to be here forever, but we have to be realistic, painfully realistic."

Julie Tarasevich, the current manager represents three generations of women managers at Straka's.

Current location of Straka's on Ann Street. The brick walls are three layers thick.

"Steam table" from which Straka's famous roast beef and pork sandwiches are served.

Detail of the tin ceiling which graces the bar and dining room.

A vintage telephone booth and modern pay phone. Many phone calls were made from this location by steel workers to their wives and girlfriends announcing that they would be coming home a little late from the 4 to 12 shift.

INTERVIEW

Jayne Kundravi, Munhall

Jayne Kundravi's home on 8th Avenue — one of, if not the, oldest house in Homestead today — has a history that pre-dates the Homestead Steel Strike of 1892.

First owner Dr. Fogelman sold the house to Dr. McNeely, who made house calls from his horse-drawn carriage — and charged 50 cents for an office visit. Dr. McNeely — well known for his ability to communicate with the immigrant population, despite language barriers, practiced until his death in the mid 1940s.

Jayne's father, Michael Kundravi Sr., bought the house after the doctor's death. Michael Sr. worked for U.S.Steel for 50 years, and his sons Tom and Michael Jr., 40 years apiece.

Jayne — who has lived in the home most of her life — is known for her festive decorations during holidays, and receives many requests for tours of her abode.

OLD-FASHIONED POTATO SOUP

5-6 medium or large potatoes,
     cleaned and quartered

1 tbl. caraway seed

1 stick margarine

salt to taste

Place potatoes and caraway seed in soup pot and cover with water. Cook until tender. Cook margarine until brown, not burnt. Add to soup for color and taste along with salt.

Mary Kundravi, Munhall

SWEET DESSERT SOUP

1/2 cup rice, cooked and drained

2 cups fresh milk warmed
     until hot (do not boil)

1 1/2 tsps. vanilla

1-2 tbls. sugar to taste

Mix ingredients in order. Delicious served with poundcake.

Mary Kundravi, Munhall

PULNINA
VEAL LOAF

1 1/2 lb.s ground veal

1 1/2 cups ground saltine crackers

3 eggs

2 tbls. fresh parsley, chopped

salt and pepper to taste

1/4 cup chopped onion

4 tbls. margarine

Cook onion in margarine until tender. Mix together all other ingredients and add cooked onion and margarine. Mix thoroughly and form two loaves of equal size. Place both loaves into a 9" x 13" covered baking dish and bake for 1 1/2 hours at 350°.

Loosen loaves with a metal pancake turner after the first 40 minutes of baking to prevent sticking. About 15 minutes before done, remove cover and allow loaves to lightly brown on the outside.

Test if done as you would a meatloaf. Remove from pan and drain on absorbent paper. Let cool, wrap and refrigerate. Serve cold, sliced or cubed. Serve on a platter with cubed Cirek, ham, kolbassi, etc. for a tasty Easter appetizer tray.

Adele Vamos, Munhall

CHRISTMAS BEAN DISH

½ lb. baby lima beans

½ lb. pinto beans

6-7 cups cold water

1 small onion, chopped

4 tbls. oil

4 tbls. flour

white vinegar

Soak beans overnight in cold water. Drain and add 6 to 7 cups cold water. Add onion and bring to a boil. Turn down to simmer and let cook for 2 to 3 hours. Stir occasionally to prevent sticking. When done fry oil with flour. Stir until brown and thick. Add to the cooked beans. When ready to serve, put 1 tsp. vinegar in each individual serving. Serves 6 to 8.

Luann Zamba, Whitaker

"This dish is part of the meal traditionally prepared every Christmas Eve. This recipe has been in my family for many years and was brought to America by my grandparents."

NUT ROLLS

1 cake yeast

1 cup milk, lukewarm

4 tbls. sugar

2 cups flour, sifted

6 eggs, separated

½ lb. butter, softened

2 tsps. salt

2 tbls. shortening

2 cups milk, scalded and cooled

or 2 cups sweet cream

1 tsp. vanilla

7 cups flour, sifted

Mix first 4 ingredients and set aside for about ½ hour. Add beaten egg yolks, butter, salt, shortening and milk or cream. Stir until well blended. Beat egg whites until firm, add vanilla and add to first mixture. Mix well and gradually add about 3 cups flour. Knead until dough is smooth and elastic. Cover with dish towel and set aside until doubled in bulk. Punch down and allow dough to rise again. Repeat this process two more times, or until dough is light. Turn out on lightly floured board and divide into six parts. Roll about ¼" thick and spread with nut or poppyseed filling. Bake at 350° for about 45 minutes.

CIREK
EASTER CHEESE

1 doz. eggs, break yolks but do   1 qt. milk
    not beat   ½ cup sugar

1-2 tsps. vanilla

Combine all ingredients in a white enamel pan. Cook over medium to low heat, stirring constantly, until eggs curdle and form a heavy curd. Pour mixture into a colander that is lined with several layers of cheesecloth or a cotton dish towel. Once drained pick it up, cheesecloth and all, and twist the top part of the cloth tight until you've formed a ball. Tightly tie the open end with string, keeping the string very close to the top of the ball. Mixture will be very hot so be careful. Hang over the sink or on a clothesline until cool. Once it is cooled and formed, remove cheesecloth, wrap and refrigerate. Serve cold, sliced or cubed, with ham and Veal Loaf (pulnina). You must have extreme patience in making this dish. It takes about one hour to heat slowly and cook.

Adele Vamos, Munhall

"This recipe has a rather bland but sweet taste indicative of the moderation that Christians should have in all things. My childhood memories of Cirek include the many households in Whitaker with Cirek balls hanging outside on clotheslines at Easter time. When I saw my baba's (grandmother's) Cirek hanging out on the line or from the spigot in the bathtub, I knew we'd be taking the Easter basket to church for the traditional blessing of the baskets on Holy Saturday."

NEW MOTHERS' BARLEY SOUP

2 cups chopped celery   3 large carrots, diced

2 large onions, chopped   ½ cup medium barley

½ stick margarine   1 tsp. salt

6-7 cup water   ½ tsp. pepper

½ cup milk   3 tbls. rice

Saute first 3 ingredients until golden brown. Add remaining ingredients. Cover and simmer slowly for 1 hour or until carrots are cooked. It will thicken slightly but if it's too thick, a little water may be added.

Marlene Nosich, Glassport

"My grandmother used to make this soup for her daughters after the birth of a child, thus the name. My own mother always claimed that barley is one of nature's perfect foods — no salt —no cholesterol and very high in fiber and protein ... the perfect food for a new mother."

CHRISTMAS MUSHROOM SOUP (SOUR)

10 oz. dried mushrooms

    (Can be purchased seasonally

    in Homestead)

12 cups cold water

 1 medium onion, chopped

 1 tsp. paprika

2 tbls. butter

1 8 oz. can sauerkraut, rinsed

   and drained, reserving liquid

1 tbl. salt

  pinch of pepper

½ cup barley

Thoroughly wash mushrooms by rinsing in cold water. Chop into small pieces. Add mushrooms to boiling water. While water is heating, saute onion and paprika in butter until browned and tender. Once the water begins to boil, add mushrooms, sauerkraut, salt, pepper and onion mixture. Turn heat to simmer and allow to cook for 3 hours. Add barley and cook an additional hour. Add a little sauerkraut juice from the reserve if you desire a more sour tasting soup. Serves 10 to 12.

Anna Mae Vamos, Whitaker

"I learned this recipe from watching my mother-in-law prepare it every year for the traditional Christmas Eve Supper. My father-in-law and husband would go mushroom hunting every fall and we dried the mushrooms on strings above the stove in their tiny kitchen. Every year I asked them the same question when they returned from their hunt: Are you sure there are no toadstools in here? But somehow they knew!"

CIBERJA
POTATO SOUP

6-8 medium potatoes

    water to fill ¾ of an 8 qt.

    soup pot

½ gal. buttermilk

 2 tbls. flour

2 eggs

  Zapruska base

1 can green or wax beans,

   drained (optional)

Peel and cut potatoes into small pieces and boil in water until soft. Have hot water on hand if needed to add to potatoes. You will want to have at least 1 qt. of water left in the soup pot when potatoes are done. Do not let potatoes become overcooked and thick.

Whip buttermilk, flour and eggs until you have a smooth mixture. When there are no lumps left in it, pour directly into the soup and stir. Add Zapruska and stir. Add beans if you are using them. Stir constantly so soup does not burn. Heat thoroughly. Serves 6 to 8.

Barbara Sturms, Duquesne

ZAPRASHKA
SAUCE AND SOUP THICKENING

This is prepared as a thickening for soups and sauces of any kind. It is customary to make it in quantity and have it on hand whenever needed. The proportions are to combine twice as much flour as shortening and fry slowly, stirring constantly until it is light brown. Pour into a small pan and when it cools, it will settle. It is ready to use without any further preparation, and lasts indefinitely without spoiling. If making a small quantity for one recipe, use 1 tbl. of shortening and 2 tbls. of flour; fry slowly a few minutes and add to recipe as called for.

Ruth Racko, White Oak

CARAWAY SEED SOUP

3 tbls. bacon fat or shortening	1 garlic clove, crushed
2 tbls. flour	salt and white pepper to taste
1 tbl. caraway seeds	2 tbls. butter
1 tbl. paprika	croutons

The medicinal properties of caraway seeds have been highly praised since ancient times, particularly by Slavic peoples. They greatly appreciate the small seed's gastronomic value and use it in many dishes.

Melt fat in a saucepan. Stir in flour to blend well. Add caraway seeds and cook 1 minute. Remove from heat and stir in paprika, garlic, salt and pepper. Mix well. Return to heat and add butter. Cook, stirring, until butter melts. Add 6 cups boiling water and cook slowly, covered, for 10 minutes. Strain and serve with croutons on top. Serves 6.

SLOVAK HALUSKY

2 eggs	2 cups flour
½ cup cold water	boiling water
1 tsp. salt	

Break eggs into a bowl, add cold water, salt and mix together. Add enough flour to make a medium stiff dough. Let it set while the water come to boil. Place dough on a small paddle-type board, cut off small pieces with table knife, dropping into boiling water. Boil gently until noodle-like dumplings rise to top of water. Cook for 5 minutes covered, but watch to keep it from boiling over. Remove from boiling water with sieve and blanch with cold water. Place in bowl with a little butter and mix lightly.

Emelia Ivaska

BUNDURCOV HALUSKI
POTATO DUMPLINGS

2 cups raw potatoes	1 tsp. salt
2 medium eggs	1 cup flour (approx.)

Finely grate potatoes. Add egg, salt, flour. Mix well to create a pasty dough. Add a little water if dough is too pasty.

Take a handful of dough, place it on a plate and chip off pieces of dough with the tip of a teaspoon into a pot of boiling water. You can test to see if they are done by cooling and tasting one or when dough takes on a shiny appearance. Rinse in hot water, drain. Mix lightly with browned butter or margarine, and dry cottage cheese and sauerkraut.

The woman who submitted this recipe wishes to remain anonymous. Born in 1917 on Hays Lane in Munhall, she worked in the mills in the early 1940s. "I started out on the labor gang pitching bricks from boxcars." The bricks were passed from person to person, hand to hand, stacked, and later used to replace the burned out bricks in the open hearth furnace.

She worked three shifts, six days a week and walked from her Munhall home, including a flight of 75 steps each way to get to her job. She still lives in her family's home, which is over 100 years old.

"It was an experience and at the same time it was a fearful job because once the furnace would burn out, different groups of people would come and clean out the furnace. They would let the furnace cool and once it cooled they were only allowed in there for a few minutes. The bricks would burn down and they wouldn't work anymore. The fire was all gas and it was under a big pot. That's what it was like. I always said that when I die I'll never go to hell because I was in hell for four years."

During her years in the mill, she said the cafeteria employed a Slovak cook. Although she did not eat lunch in the cafeteria, she did know that they served a lot of haluski and soups such as bean or mushroom.

INTERVIEW

Stephen M. Vamos, Whitaker

Stephen Vamos who worked for U.S. Steel for 36 years, remembers his family making sausage when he was six years old in 1927.

"In those days, a couple of families would go in together and purchase a pig from someone's farm or the slaughter house. The cleaning and distributing of the pig was a festive event. First they'd burn the hair off of the pig and scrape the skin with a sharp knife. Every single part of the pig was used for some dish, including the feet, blood, and organs. The children gathered around for a special treat — a piece of the pig's ear or tail to chew on! Someone in the neighborhood usually had a smokehouse and they'd let you store your meat in there if your family didn't have one."

Original kitchen tools used to make homemade kolbassi brought from the old country by Helen and Stephen Vamos.

HOMEMADE KOLBASSI

5 lbs. pork butts	1 tsp. pepper
2 cloves garlic, finely chopped	casings, enough to use
2 tbls. salt	up prepared meat

Grind meat in coarse grinder and mix well with other ingredients. Stuff cleaned casings with meat mixture. Some local markets carry cleaned, prepackaged casings around the Easter season. Put in smokehouse and smoke daily for about a week, using hickory wood. A temporary smoke house can be made from a large tin drum.

Stephen M. Vamos, Whitaker

PIROHY

1 cup flour	4-5 tbls. water
1 egg	2-3 tbls. butter
pinch of salt	

Combine all ingredients to make a medium soft dough. Knead well. Roll dough out thin and cut into 2" squares. Put a little of any desired filling on each square and fold to form a triangle. Pinch edges together to keep filling in. Drop into boiling salted water and cook until all rise to top. Cook additional 5 minutes. Drain and place in serving bowl. Brown butter and pour over cooked pirohy. Mix lightly until all are buttered. Serve hot.

Cottage Cheese

Combine:

1/2 cup dry cottage cheese	1 tbl. sugar
1 egg yolk	

Sauerkraut

Drain and wash kraut, and parboil about 10 minutes. Drain and squeeze dry. Saute 1 medium onion in butter. Add sauerkraut, salt to taste and brown.

Potato

Blend together:

1 potato, cooked and mashed	salt
	yellow cheese, grated

Mrs. Margaret Majercik

HOLUBKY
STUFFED CABBAGE

1 lb. ground beef and pork	salt and pepper to taste
½ cup rice, cooked in boiling water 8 minutes, drained	4 lb. loose head cabbage
	1 large can sauerkraut
1 egg	1 medium can tomatoes

Combine ground meat, rice, egg and seasoning. Core cabbage and parboil about 20 minutes covered. Separate leaves. When cool, stuff with meat mixture and roll up. In large kettle place a layer of sauerkraut, a layer of cabbage rolls, then a layer of tomatoes, seasoning as you go. When all is used, cover to the top of the kettle with boiling water and cook over medium heat about 2 ½ hours.

SLOVAK GOULASH

1 medium onion, chopped	1 tsp. paprika
3 tbls. butter	1 tsp. caraway seeds
1 lb. beet and/or veal, cut into 1" cubes	2 cups water
	2 carrots, diced
1 tsp. salt	3 large potatoes, cubed
1 tsp. pepper	1 green pepper, chopped

Brown onion in butter and add cubes of meat. Simmer slowly until golden brown. Add salt, pepper, paprika, caraway seeds and enough water to cover the meat. Let goulash simmer for 1 hour or until meat is tender. Add water if necessary to keep meat in sauce. Add carrots, potatoes and green pepper and continue until vegetables are done. Serves 6.

Ethel Kochuliak Lovelace

SAUERKRAUT RELISH

1 jar or 1 #2 ½ can sauerkraut, drained and squeezed	1 cup celery, finely chopped
	1 ½ cup granulated sugar
1 medium onion, finely chopped	½ cup oil
	⅔ cup vinegar
1 green pepper, finely chopped	⅓ cup water

Mix together; let stand overnight. Pimento or red pepper may be added for color.

Virginia Ursin

KOCHANINA
JELLIED PIGS FEET

3 lbs. pigs feet, each chopped in
   half lengthwise

1 tbl. salt

water

$\frac{1}{8}$ tsp pepper

$\frac{1}{4}$ tsp sweet paprika, optional

2 cloves garlic

Singe pigs feet, wash and boil. Pour off water. Add fresh water, just enough to cover. Bring to boiling point, skim, if necessary. Simmer slowly. Add next 3 ingredients. Cook until bones fall apart, about 4 to 5 hours. Pour into soup plates and let stand overnight in a cold place.

Adele Vamos, Munhall

CRANBERRY/RASPBERRY/SOUR CREAM MOLD

1 6 oz. package raspberry
   gelatin

1 $\frac{3}{4}$ cups boiling water

1 16 oz. can cranberry sauce

1 20 oz. can crushed pineapple,
   undrained

1 cup dairy sour cream

Dissolve gelatin in boiling water. Stir in cranberry sauce and undrained pineapple until cranberry sauce melts. Chill till partially set. Pour half of the mixture into a 6 $\frac{1}{2}$ cup ring mold. Chill until almost firm. Let remaining gelatin stand at room temperature. Stir sour cream, spread evenly over gelatin in mold. Gently spoon remaining gelatin mixture on top of sour cream layer. Chill until firm, several hours or overnight. Makes 12 servings.

Ann Richards

COLD DOUGH

8 cups flour

12 egg yolks, beaten

1 $\frac{1}{2}$ lbs. butter

1 tsp. salt

2 oz. yeast

$\frac{1}{4}$ cup lukewarm milk

1 pt. sour cream

1 oz. whiskey

Work flour, salt and butter as for pie crust. Crumble yeast in lukewarm milk and dissolve. Add yeast, beaten egg yolks and sour cream to flour mixture. Knead well until smooth. Refrigerate overnight. Roll out on flour and sugar on board. Cut into squares and fill with favorite filling. Roll and bake 18 to 20 minutes in 375° oven.

Margaret Majercik

PALACINKY
CREPES

4 eggs	1 1/2 cups milk
3 tsps. sugar	2 cups flour
1/2 tsp. salt	1 tbl. melted shortening

Separate yolks and whites of the eggs. To the beaten eggs, add the sugar, salt and 1/2 cup milk. Stir in the sifted flour and the rest of the milk and shortening. Beat well. Then fold in the stiffly beaten egg whites. Bake on a hot griddle as a pancake, but spread very thin. Spread with prune filling, jelly or cottage cheese. Roll up and place into a buttered baking dish. Sprinkle sugar and a little cream over the top. Bake for 20 minutes at 350°.

Ann Richards

CHEREGIE

7 1/2 cups flour	1/2 tsp. salt	
1 1/2 cups sugar	1/4 lb. butter	
2 1/2 tsps. baking powder	1/4 lb. margarine	
2 1/2 tsps. baking soda		

Mix the above ingredients well.
Beat the following ingredients well and add to above:

9 eggs	1/2 tsp. vanilla
1 pt. buttermilk	1/2 cup ginger ale
1/4 pt. sour cream	

Roll out to thin dough. Cut into squares or triangles. Make a slit through the center from corner to corner and pull one end of square through. Deep fry these in hot shortening until delicately browned. When done and drained, sprinkle with powdered sugar.

Helen Bartos

BUBLANINA
CHERRY OR BLUEBERRY SQUARES

½ cup butter	2 egg whites, stiffly beaten
½ cup sugar	½ tsp. lemon peel
2 egg yolks, beaten	½ tsp. cream of tartar
1 cup flour	1 lb. fresh blueberries or sweet
½ teaspoon salt	or sour cherries, pitted

Cream the butter with the sugar. Add beaten yolks to butter-sugar mixture and blend until smooth. Sift flour and salt together. Fold into creamed mixture alternately with stiffly beaten egg whites, beginning and ending with flour. Fold in lemon peel and cream of tartar. Spoon batter into a greased and floured 10" x 6" x 1 ½" baking dish and spread evenly over bottom of pan. Sprinkle berries with flour so they will not fall to the bottom. Place fruit on top of batter. Sprinkle with sugar, if desired. Bake in preheated 400° oven for 35 to 40 minutes. To serve cut into squares. Yield: 15 servings.

Millicent Bibza Skarzynski

KOLACHKY

1 cup milk, scalded	1 small yeast
½ cup sugar	4 cups flour
1 cup shortening	4 eggs
(½ butter - ½ margarine)	

Combine first 3 ingredients and cool to lukewarm. Add yeast and stir well with wooden spoon. Add flour alternately with eggs. Stir well after each addition. Let rise for 6 hours in cool place, not refrigerator. Roll out about ½" thick. Cut into 3" squares and fill with favorite fillings, such as prune, cottage cheese, apricot or canned pie fillings. Place on greased pans and let rise for 1 hour. Bake at 375° until brown, about 18-20 minutes. Brush with melted butter when removed from oven. Cool slightly and ice with powdered sugar icing or just sprinkle with powdered sugar when cool.

Margaret Majercik

(Ko-lach-key)
There are many ethnic versions of the word Kolachki, Kolachky, Rohlicky, Kolaczki, Kolacki, Kolache, Rozky. The prefix Ko or Ro comes from an ancient language base meaning — roll, horn or stem.

WORLD WAR II

For 8,000 Homestead residents the war really hit home in 1941. To better serve the nation as "patriots", they had to give up their homes and the only community many immigrants of Lower Homestead — called "The Ward" — had ever known.

In June 1941, the area in Homestead between the railroad tracks and the river was designated for the country's largest war-time steel-making expansion, connecting the Homestead and Munhall mill sites. The bitter flavor of the Depression still in the back of industry's throat, U.S. Steel jumped at the $86 million government contract.

To some, the arranged migration meant new jobs and improved infrastructure, to others it generated fear, confusion and resentment.

In the end, it took six months to dismantle a way of life that had taken a century to build, says Chris Miner and Paul Roberts in *Engineering an Industrial Diaspora: Homestead 1941*. One thousand three hundred sixty-three buildings, 12 churches, five schools, two convents and innumerable small businesses and fraternal organizations were sacrificed to the 121-acre site while most of the people were transferred to government housing. Within three years Lower Homestead metamorphosized from an immigrant neighborhood with its own culture and history, into one of the most formidable manufacturing sites of the second World War.

Surpassing the Great War's copious manufacturing levels, Pittsburgh's industrial production was up 186.8 percent in the first year of the war, with its steel output more than doubling for 1939. While established factories produced a staggering 95 million tons of Pittsburgh steel and $19 billion in ammunition in the four war years, the city also added a new industry to its repertoire. Shipbuilding plants on Neville Island constructed hundreds of destroyers that traveled down the Ohio and Mississippi, out to the Gulf and across the ocean to the European war front.

The labor shortage became so critical recruiters were sent to homes to try to secure women volunteers, after approximately 25 percent of the production workforce was already female. In 1941 5,000 housing units in West Mifflin, Pittsburgh, Munhall, and Glen Hazel, were being constructed for war workers, more than anywhere else in the country.

NEW ENGLAND CHOWDER

⅔ cup salt pork (fat back),
   diced into small pieces

⅔ cup sliced onions

3 cups sliced potatoes

1 tsp. salt

¼ tsp. pepper

1 cup water

1 cup milk

2 lbs. lean fish (cod or haddock
   are best, however, any lean
   fish may be used)

In a heavy kettle or Dutch oven, fry the pork to a golden brown color, add onions and fry these to a light yellow color. Add potatoes, sprinkle with salt and pepper, add the water and milk, and cook until the potatoes are soft. Remove any skin from the fish and break the flesh into coarse flakes. More liquid may be needed as the chowder cooks. Add equal parts of milk and water for any desired consistency.

The Daily Messenger, July 24, 1942

CREAM OF FISH SOUP

Cut 1 pound of fish into pieces. Add 4 cups cold water, 4 pepper-corns and a bunch of soup greens. Bring to a boil; simmer 40 minutes. Strain. Add water to stock to make 1 quart. Melt 3 tablespoons butter, add 3 tablespoons flour. When boiling stir in the soup stock. Bring to boiling point. Add 1 cup green peas, 2 cups diced carrots, 1 cup diced potato and season to taste. When cooked, add 2 cups hot milk.

The Daily Messenger, July 24, 1942

CLAM CHOWDER
MANHATTAN STYLE

1/4	lb. salt pork	4	cups water
2	large onions, chopped		pinch of thyme
1	carrot diced		salt and pepper
1	cup celery, diced	2	doz. large clams,
1	green pepper, diced		finely chopped
2	cups tomato pulp		hot clam liquor

Dice and brown salt pork. Remove from pan. Saute in pork fat until beginning to brown, then add the next 4 ingredients. Add tomatoes, water, and seasonings. Cook for 10 minutes. Add clams. Simmer until tender. Add hot clam liquor. Thicken with crackers or pilot biscuits.

The Daily Messenger, July 24, 1942

FISH FLAKE OMELETTE

3	tbls. vinegar or lemon juice	1/2	cup milk or fish stock
2	cups flaked cooked fish	1	tsp. salt
4	tbls. melted butter	1/4	tsp. black pepper
	or cooking oil	2	tbls. chopped parsley
4	eggs	2	tbls. grated onion

Add the vinegar or lemon juice to fish flakes. Heat butter slowly in frying pan. Beat egg whites stiff and set aside. Beat egg yolks, add milk or stock, salt, pepper, parsley, onion and stir. Add cold flakes and mix well. Last fold in stiff egg whites and pour into hot fat in frying pan. Cook slowly over low heat until cooked through. Place in heated oven to dry on top. When dry enough to touch without wetting fingers remove and cut opposite edges loose from pan. Fold over and remove to hot platter.

The Daily Messenger, July 17, 1942

SUPPER CHEESE CASSEROLE

12	slices day-old bread	3	cups milk
1/3	cup butter or margarine	1/2	tsp. salt
2	cups grated American cheese	1	tsp. Worcestershire Sauce
3	eggs, slightly beaten		paprika

Spread bread slices with butter or margarine. Place a layer of 6 slices in a large shallow, greased baking dish, and sprinkle heavily with grated cheese. Repeat process, making 2 layers. Combine beaten eggs with milk, salt and Worcestershire sauce and pour over bread and cheese. Sprinkle with paprika. Place baking dish in pan of hot water and bake in moderately slow oven (325°) 1 1/4 hours until set. Serve hot. Serves 6 to 8.

The Daily Messenger, July 14, 1942

50 Years Ago
April 24, 1942 - A survey of water consumption in major U.S. cities showed that Pittsburgh had the second highest flat rate for residential water fees — $1.53 a month, second only to Baltimore.
Pittsburgh Press, April 24, 1992

MACARONI LUNCHEONETTE

2	cups cooked macaroni		juice of one large lemon
1	large can shrimp	1	cup mayonnaise
1	avocado		paprika
2	hard-cooked eggs		

Put cooked macaroni in a colander and pour cold water through it to separate it thoroughly. Remove black outer line from shrimp and cut in two. Peel avocado and dice, also dice the whites of the cooked eggs. Moisten the yolks of eggs with lemon juice and mayonnaise. Stir the whole together and serve on lettuce leaf, topping each portion with spoonful of mayonnaise liberally sprinkled with paprika.

The Daily Messenger, July 14, 1942

HAM AND GREEN TOMATO GRILL

green tomatoes	salt
boiled ham, sliced ¼" thick	bread crumbs
rich brown prepared mustard	butter

Slice tomatoes thick. Cut ham into pieces about size of tomato slices. Spread ham with the prepared mustard. Top with slice of tomato: season with salt, sprinkle with crumbs; dot top with butter and grill under low flame until tomato is cooked.

The Daily Messenger, July 24, 1942

BAKED VEAL CROQUETTES

½ cup real mayonnaise	2 tbls. water
½ tsp. salt	2 cups chopped cooked veal
⅛ tsp. pepper	1 cup fine soft bread crumbs
1 tsp. grated onion	or cooked rice
1 tsp. Worcestershire Sauce	fine dry bread crumbs
1 tbl. minced parsley	

Combine real mayonnaise and seasonings in bowl. Gradually stir in water. Add veal and soft bread crumbs or rice. Mix with fork, let stand 5 minutes. Shape into croquettes and roll in dry bread crumbs. Place ½" apart on ungreased baking sheet, lined with heavy brown paper. Bake in hot over (450°) 15-20 minutes, or until browned. Makes about 10-12 croquettes.

The Daily Messenger, July 17, 1942

LAMB EN BROCHETTE

Lamb en brochette is appropriate for kitchen or grill cooked meals. To serve six persons buy 1 ½ lbs. of lamb steak cut from shoulder or leg, about ½" thick Slice a slender cucumber in ½" rounds and place alternate pieces of lamb cut in inch squares and cucumber on skewers. Sprinkle with salt, spread thickly with prepared mustard and roll in crumbs. Broil under moderate heat turning frequently.

The Daily Messenger, July 10, 1942

BUNNY BURGERS

1 lb. hamburger meat	2 tsps. prepared mustard
1 tbl. minced onion	¾ cup freshly grated American
3 tbls. minced sweet pickle	cheese
½ tsp. salt	8 slices enriched bread
⅛ tsp. pepper	softened butter

Combine hamburger, onion, pickle and seasoning and form mixture into 8 thin flat rounds. Broil quickly on one side; turn. Spread uncooked side with mustard and sprinkle with grated cheese. Continue broiling until cheese is melted and bubbly. Toast enriched bread, spread slices with softened butter and place a bunny-burger on each. Hamburger rolls split, toasted and buttered may be used in place of toast. Serve hot with cole slaw as a garnish if desired.

The Daily Messenger, July 24, 1942

LIVER AND BACON SPECIAL

½ lb. cooked liver	6 slices enriched bread
1 tbl. minced onion	softened butter
2 tbls. mayonnaise	12 slices tomato
¼ tsp. salt	6 thin slices bacon
⅛ tsp. pepper	

Put cooked liver (either calves, lamb, beef or pork) through food chopper, or chop finely. Combine with onion, mayonnaise, salt and pepper. Toast enriched bread and spread with softened butter, then with liver mixture. Top each slice with two slices tomato. Cut bacon strips in halves and place 1 piece on top of each tomato slice. Slide sandwiches under broiler to cook bacon, about 1 minute.

The Daily Messenger, July 24, 1942

HOT HAM ROLL

½ lb. ground, cooked ham	2 cups sifted flour
1 tbl. minced onion	3 tsps. baking powder
1 tbl. minced parsley	1 tsp. salt
2 tbls. dry mustard	4 tbls. shortening
1 tbl. milk	¼ cup milk (about)

Mix ham, onion, parsley, mustard and milk together. Sift flour, baking powder, salt together. Cut or rub in shortening. Add milk to form soft biscuit dough. Roll dough out into rectangular sheet ¼" thick. Spread ham mixture on biscuit dough. Roll jelly-roll fashion to seal edge. Bake on baking sheet in moderately hot oven (425°) 20 to 25 minutes. Slice and serve hot with horseradish sauce. Serves 8.

The Daily Messenger, July 17, 1942

VEGETABLE CHOP SUEY

1 large onion	1 cup peas
small head cauliflower	1 cup boiling salted water
1 green pepper	4 tbls. vitaminized margarine
3 cups celery, diced	½ cup parsley sprigs
1 cup string beans	

Peel onion. Separate cauliflower in flowerets. Shred or slice green pepper, onion, cauliflower, celery and string beans. Cook all vegetables together except parsley in boiling salted water 15 minutes or until tender. Add vitaminized margarine. Turn into serving dish and sprinkle with parsley. Serves 6.

The Daily Messenger, July 24, 1942

CHOW MEIN

1 lb. lean pork, veal or chicken,	2 tbls. cornstarch
diced	2 cups canned bean sprouts
⅓ cup cooking fat	2 tbls. Chinese soy sauce
2 cups water or meat stock	salt and pepper
2 cups diced celery	2 cups chow mein noodles
½ cup diced onions	

Fry meat until brown in cooking fat. Add water or stock, cover and simmer until meat is tender. Add celery and onion. Simmer 10 minutes. Moisten cornstarch in a little water. Add to meat mixture, stirring until slightly thickened. Add bean sprouts and soy sauce. Season to taste with salt and pepper. Heat thoroughly and serve over noodles which have been crisped in oven.

The Daily Messenger, July 10, 1942

Safflower, a plant much like flax, has become an important farm crop in Montana. It is crushed up and makes an oil for use in paints and varnishes, much like linseed oil.
The Daily Messenger, July 24, 1942

BREAD SAUCE
FOR SCALLOPING LEFT-OVER VEGETABLES

²/₃ cup milk   2 tsps. butter

²/₃ cup soft bread crumbs   salt and pepper

Scald milk, add bread crumbs and cook over low flame, stirring until mixture thickens. Add butter, seasonings, and beat until smooth.

The Daily Messenger, July 17, 1942

Every homemaker, eager to participate in food conservation as her part in the national war effort, is learning new tricks with leftovers as fast as she can. Leftover cooked vegetables often can be stretched for another meal by scalloping with bread crumbs. Arrange 1 to 2 cups of cook vegetables in a greased baking dish in alternate layers with Bread Sauce (see recipe above), top with a layer of buttered crumbs (¹/₂ cup fine dry bread crumbs combined with 2 tablespoons melted butter). Bake in hot over (400°) until vegetables are heated and top crumbs are browned.
The Daily Messenger, July 17, 1942

POTATOES WITH SAVORY SAUCE

4 potatoes, cut in strips   2 tsps. salt

2 small onions, cut in rings   ¹/₄ tsp. pepper

4 tbls. vitaminized margarine   2 tbls. pimiento, chopped

2 tbls. flour   grated cheese

1 cup milk

Cut the raw, pared potatoes into long match-like strips. Cook them in boiling water until tender. Drain and turn into a warm dish. Brown the onion rings in the vitaminized margarine. Add the flour, stirring thoroughly; add milk, salt, pepper and pimiento and cook in double boiler 20 minutes. Pour over cooked potatoes. Sprinkle with grated cheese and serve.

The Daily Messenger, July 24, 1942

Rapid boiling is the general rule for vegetables and all scum that rises should be removed. When done drain at once, or the vegetables will lose much of their flavor.
Homestead Local News, December 15, 1893

LIMA BEANS PARISIENNE

Melt 4 tbls. vitaminized margarine in double boiler, add 4 tbls. flour and mix well. Add 1 cup milk, 1/4 cup bean stock and 1/4 cup celery stock gradually until thickened. Season with 1/2 tsp. salt and 1/8 tsp. pepper. Add 1 cup grated American cheese, 3 cups cooked Lima beans, salted, and 1 cup cooked celery, diced and salted. Mix well. Sprinkle with paprika. Serves 6.

The Daily Messenger, July 24, 1942

The water in which green peas has been boiled should not be thrown away. It has a fine flavor — the very essence of peas. A little stock added, seasoned to taste, makes an economical, delicious wholesome and appetizing soup.
Homestead Local News, December 15, 1893

FRUIT TREATS

Sift together 2 cups sifted enriched flour, 3 tsps. baking powder and 1 tsp. salt. Cut or rub in 2 to 4 tbls. shortening. Beat 1 whole egg and 1 egg yolk, reserving white for tops. Add about 1/2 cup milk and 1 tbl. honey or corn syrup to beaten eggs and add all to flour mixture. Stir only enough to make dough hold together. Turn out on lightly floured board and knead 1/2 minute. Roll out 1/2" thick, and cut with doughnut cutter. Place on baking sheet and drop an apricot or prune in the hole of each biscuit. Brush with egg white and sprinkle biscuits with cinnamon sugar, which is made by mixing 3 tbls. sugar and 1/2 tsp. cinnamon together. Bake in hot oven (425°) 12 to 15 minutes. Makes about 12 Fruit Treats.

The Daily Messenger, July 17, 1942

HONEY-BUTTER ROLL-UPS

2 cups sifted enriched flour	2/3-3/4 cup milk
3 tsps. baking powder	1 tbl. melted butter
1 tsp. salt	2 tbls. honey
4 tbls. shortening	1/2 tsp. cinnamon

Sift together first three ingredients. Cut or rub in shortening. Add milk and stir to form a soft dough. Turn out on lightly floured board and knead 1/2 minute. Divide into 2 equal portions. Roll each portion out into circular shape about 1/4" thick. Brush with melted butter and honey. Sprinkle with cinnamon. Cut into pie-shaped pieces. Roll up beginning at the wide end. Bake in hot oven (450°) 10-12 minutes. Makes about 16 roll-ups.

The Daily Messenger, July 17, 1942

PEACH SURPRISE PIE

2 cups sliced fresh peaches	3 egg whites
1/4 cup sugar	1 tsp. lemon juice
1 baked pie shell	1/8 tsp. salt
1 pt. peach ice cream	6 tbls. sugar

Slice peaches and sprinkle with a few drops of lemon juice to prevent them from turning dark. Add sugar and allow to stand for 1/2 hour before using. Place a layer of peaches in pie shell; cover this with ice cream; add more peaches and cover all with a meringue. To make meringue, beat egg whites with rotary beater until foamy; add lemon juice and salt. Continue beating until thick, then add the 6 tbls. of sugar, 2 tbls. at a time. Beat until mixture will hold its shape. Place meringue covered pie in a hot oven (500°) for 3 to 4 minutes. Serve at once. Serves 6

The Daily Messenger, July 24, 1942

FRESH PEACH FLOATING ISLAND

2 tbls. cornstarch	1/2 tsp. vanilla
1/4 tsp. salt	few drops almond extract
4 tbls. sugar	1/4 tsp. ground nutmeg
2 egg yolks	2 cups sliced fresh peaches
1 pt. hot milk	meringue crown

Combine cornstarch, salt and sugar. Add milk gradually and cook in a double boiler, stirring constantly until slightly thickened. Beat egg yolks slightly. Pour hot milk over them slowly. Cook in double boiler until custard coats spoon. Cool. Add flavorings. Pour into shallow serving dish. Add one cup of the fruit. Chill. Just before serving top with meringue crown and fill with remaining fruit. This will serve 4.

To make meringue crown beat 3 egg whites until stiff but not dry. Add 6 tbls. sugar and pinch of salt gradually, beating continuously. Pile meringue in greased 9" pie plate. Set in shallow pan of water. Bake in moderate oven (325°) 20 minutes. Cool.

The Daily Messenger, July 24, 1942

ITALIANS

Part of the southern and eastern European wave, Italians began leaving their homes in the latter 1800s for opportunities in North and South America. The earlier part of the century saw the transfer of land in southern Italy from peasants to wealthy land owners, leaving few opportunities short of working as farm laborers — a role that moved southern Italians away from their agrarian roots into more self-sufficient trades.

Intent on proprietorship and social mobility, Italians came to western Pennsylvania with little thought of returning to Abruzzi, Puglia, Calabria or other regions of the Mezzogiorno they left behind. Skills learned to supplement seasonal income provided immigrants with experience as peddlers, masons, shoemakers, carpenters and tailors that enabled many start their own businesses. Others found work as laborers in mines, construction and on railroads. They were earning $11.90 a week in the mills by 1910.

By the early 1880s a constant stream of Italians — primarily from Abruzzi towns like Ateleta, Castel di Sangro and Pesco Costanza — settled into a four block area of downtown Pittsburgh between Smithfield and Grant Streets. Growth moved Italians outward, to the Hill District, Bloomfield and East Liberty. Many immigrants found employment in the latter neighborhood's newly built filtration plant in 1905 and it was again in that part of the East End the first Italian Catholic church was established in 1897.

Italian neighborhoods radiated a strong sense of kinship, paving the way for other immigrants. That unity has kept Bloomfield one of Pittsburgh's ethnic strongholds to this day.

INTERVIEW

Ed and Alice Manfredi, West Mifflin

Ed worked in the steel industry for a total of 38 years. "I started at U.S. Steel, Homestead Works, in 1945 until I enlisted into the army a year later. When I returned from the service, I began working for Jones & Laughlin Steel in Hays until my retirement in 1987".

Ed's parents emigrated from Italy bringing their unique ways of cooking with them. Ed preferred to take "leftovers" or last night's dinner in his lunch. "I carried them in plastic containers and heated them in pots and pans they kept in the mill right on the furnace. Often other steelworkers would bring food in and there would be group cooking. The cafeteria was one quarter of a mile away from where I worked so because of the 30 minute time allotted I didn't us the cafeteria". Perhaps the money steelworkers saved over the years by carrying their lunches in from home, went to a greater cause ... the less fortunate. "Steelworkers were paid in cash back then. There were pay stations set up in the courtyard near the OH4, popularly known as "the hole in the wall". On paydays, we would walk up City Farm Lane with our pay envelopes. As we walked passed the nuns we would turn our envelopes upside down and dump the loose change into their collection boxes."

Alice, born of German and French descent, was raised in a family of 11 children in Homestead's Second Ward. Over time Alice incorporated her knowledge of cooking with the Manfredi family's Italian influence to create some wonderful dinners (and tomorrow's lunches) for 38 years.

ITALIAN BRACIOLA
ROUND STEAK ROLL

2 tbls. chopped parsley	1 tsp. black pepper
2 tbls. fresh chopped garlic	1 large, thin round steak
2 tbls. Italian grated cheese	(no fat)
2 tbls. bread crumbs	hard boiled eggs

Combine the first 5 ingredients. Cut the round steak in 3 or 4 nice slices. Cut the steak large so you can roll the egg in it. About 3" or 4" long. On each slice of steak, spread the above mixture and put hard boiled egg in the middle of the slice. Roll the meat up like nut roll or cabbage roll. Tie the meat roll with string. Brown the pan with olive oil. Cook the steaks with tomato sauce or spaghetti sauce until tender, about 1 hour. After the meat is cooked and cooled, remove the string. Slice down like a pinwheel. Serve with sauce and grated cheese on top.

Alice Manfredi, West Mifflin

FETTUNTA
REAL ITALIAN GARLIC BREAD

Grill thick slices of salt-less Italian bread over a bright fire until golden crisp on the outside but still soft within. Rub fat cloves of raw garlic (cut in half) over bread. Laying the slices on a large plate, they are drizzled with warm olive oil and sprinkled with a good pinch of coarse salt.

Pat Sommers, Munhall

EGG AND SPINACH SOUP

4 cups broth	4 eggs
1 ½ lbs. fresh spinach, without	½ cup grated Parmesan
stems *	salt and pepper to taste

Bring broth to a boil and add spinach. Cook for 5 minutes. Beat eggs with 1 tbl. cheese. Pour into simmering soup. Simmer 1 minute. Top each serving with more cheese. Serve with garlic bread.
* Peas may be used instead of spinach.

Pat Sommers, Munhall

PASTE E FAGIOLI
PEASANT BEAN SOUP

1 cup white beans, soaked overnight	1 tbl. tomato paste, diluted in ⅓ cup water
1 beef marrow bone, about 5" long	1 cup detalini macaroni
¼ cup olive oil	⅓ tsp. rosemary
2 cloves garlic	1 tbl. flour
2 tbls. parsley	salt and pepper

Cook beans and bone in 3 ½ quarts of cold water for 1 ½ hours, covered. Meanwhile saute garlic, parsley and rosemary in oil. Add flour, stirring constantly. Simmer 6 minutes. Add tomato paste and water mixture and cook 10 minutes. Remove garlic, add sauce to beans and simmer 2 hours more. Add more water if soup is too thick. Add macaroni, cook 10 to 12 minutes more, stirring occasionally. Let stand 20 minutes, then serve with garlic bread. Serve Parmesan on the side. Very inexpensive and delicious.

Pat Sommers, Munhall

MINESTRONE

½ cup olive oil	2 tsps. salt
1 clove garlic, minced	¼ tsp. pepper
2 cups chopped onion	⅛ tsp. sage
1 cup chopped celery	1 1 lb. can kidney beans
4 tbls. chopped parsley	1 zucchini squash, thinly sliced
1 can tomato paste	
1 10 ½ oz. can beef broth	1 cup frozen or canned green beans
9 cups water	
1 cup coarsely chopped cabbage	1 cup elbow macaroni
2 carrots, thinly sliced	Parmesan cheese, grate

Heat oil in large pot. Add first 4 ingredients. Cook until soft. Stir in tomato paste and next 7 ingredients. Mix well and bring to a boil. Lower heat, cover and simmer slowly for 1 hour. Add remaining ingredients except cheese. Cook 10 to 15 minutes more or until macaroni is tender. Serve piping hot with plenty of cheese.

Rose Bikulege, Dormont

WEDDING SOUP

3 bouillon cubes	1 onion, diced
1 gallon water	1 whole carrot
1 lb. chicken breasts	1 stalk celery
1 clove garlic, minced	fresh parsley

Combine all ingredients in large soup pot. Note: Once meat is cooked, it should be broken into small pieces. Also, the carrot and celery should be removed at this point.

Small Meatballs
(size of large marble)

1 lb. ground turkey or chicken	1/4 cup Romano or Parmesan
1 cup Italian bread crumbs	fresh parsley
1 egg	1 small onion, minced
1 clove garlic, minced	1/2 tsp. basil, fresh or dried

Roll meatballs and place on cookie sheet lined with foil. Bake in 500° oven until cooked. Watch closely and turn once. (They can be frozen). Add meatballs to soup along with:

1/2 cup acine pi pi or	1 lb. escarole or endive,
Rosemarie pasta	cleaned and chopped

Simmer for 1 hour.

Carmella Wergryn, West Mifflin

FRESH TOMATO AND ZUCCHINI SAUCE

3 lbs. fresh tomatoes	3 cups shredded zucchini
2 tbls. salad oil	(2 medium)
1/2 cup chopped onion	1 tsp. salt
1/2 tsp. minced garlic	1/2 tsp. thyme
	1/8 tsp. black pepper

Use fully ripe tomatoes. Seed and chop tomatoes to make about 5 1/2 cups. Heat oil in medium saucepan. Add onion and garlic and saute for 5 minutes. Add remaining ingredients and simmer (covered) for 15 minutes, stirring occasionally. Serve over fresh green beans, pasta, rice or broccoli spears.

Adele Buck, Penn Hills

ITALIANS

SPAGHETTI SAUCE

1 large or 2 medium onions	1 tsp. oregano
3 tbls. olive oil	½ tsp. basil
2 cloves garlic	½ tsp. Italian seasoning
1 ¼ lbs. ground meat, lean	red crushed pepper to taste
1 29 oz. can tomato puree	4 bay leaves
½ above can of water	1 tsp. sugar
1 12 oz. can tomato paste	1 tbl. Worcestershire sauce
½ above can of water	½ cup red wine
2 tsps. salt	¼ cup Parmesan cheese
½ tsp. pepper	

Saute first 4 ingredients until all red is out of the meat. Add remaining ingredients and mix thoroughly. Simmer for 2 hours.

Shirley Kann, Monroeville

POTATO GNOCCHI

3 lbs. potatoes (5 or 6 large)	1 egg
3 tbls. grated Parmesan	salt and pepper to taste
3 cups flour (scant)	

Boil potatoes in salted water and drain. Put in bowl and mash. Add cheese, flour, egg and seasoning. Roll and form. Drop in boiling water. They will surface when cooked. Remove them with a slotted spoon and serve with your favorite sauce.

Adele Buck, Penn Hills

LINGUINI WITH BROCCOLI ALA ROMANO

1 bunch fresh broccoli	1 cup grated Parmesan cheese
1 clove garlic	1 lb. linguini, cooked and
⅓ cup olive oil	drained

Trim away three to four inches of broccoli stems and discard. Cook broccoli in boiling salted water. Remove while still firm. Saute mashed garlic in olive oil until golden. Remove garlic. Add broccoli and saute 10 minutes, stirring to brown pieces lightly. Season to taste. Toss broccoli with hot linguini and Parmesan cheese. Serve immediately.

Alice Manfredi, West Mifflin

GNOCCHI WITH BROCCOLI

1 lb. gnocchi	salt and pepper to taste
½ cup olive oil	10 oz. frozen chopped broccoli
¼ lb. butter	Parmesan cheese, grated
1-2 cloves garlic	

Defrost broccoli and drain well. Cook gnocchi. Meanwhile, heat the oil and butter in saucepan the saute garlic until light brown. (You may discard garlic.) Add drained broccoli and heat until warm. Turn gnocchi into bowl and toss oil/broccoli mixture with gnocchi and top with cheese then toss again.

Adele Buck, Penn Hills

FETTUCCINI WITH SPINACH AND CHEESE

½ lb. fresh spinach	8 ozs. fettuccini (medium egg
1 clove garlic, mashed	noodles)
2 tbls. chopped onion	½ cup heavy cream
½ cup butter or margarine	1 cup grated Parmesan cheese
	freshly ground black pepper

Remove and discard tough stems from spinach, tear or coarsely chop leaves. In pan, cook garlic and onion in half the butter until golden. Add spinach, cover and cook until just wilted. Meanwhile, cook noodles as directed on package, drain and mix with remaining butter. Then toss with cream cheese and spinach. Sprinkle with pepper. Makes 3 to 4 servings.

Shirley Kann, Monroeville

FETTUCCINI WITH BACON

¼ lb. bacon,	½ cup heavy cream
very crisp and crumbled	½ cup Parmesan cheese
1 box (12 oz.) fettuccini,	2 eggs, slightly beaten
cooked and drained	2 parsley tops, snipped
¼ cup butter	salt and pepper to taste

Toss well.

Shirley Kann, Monroeville

ITALIANS

GRANDPA PACITTI'S NOODLES

1 lb. Penne noodles	2 cups Half and Half cream*
1 heaping cup shredded moz-	1/4 cup grated Parmesan cheese
zarella cheese	1 tsp. salt
6 tbls. butter, softened	1/4 tsp. pepper

Cook noodles as directed. Drain well and return to same pot. Add butter, salt and pepper. Mix in grated cheese and mozzarella. Add Half and Half. Immediately transfer to large glass pan. Bake in 375° oven for 35 to 45 minutes. (Occasionally I don't move fast enough and cheese lumps into a ball. Just return pan with noodle mixture to low heat and stir, stir, stir ... it will blend beautifully, then transfer to casserole for oven.)

* I prefer Half and Half cream method, which when combined with cheese thickens beautifully. However, 2 eggs and same amount of milk is more economical and works well.

Kathie Buck, Penn Hills

"My father used to carry his lunch wrapped in newspapers as lunch bags and lunch boxes were nonexistent. He worked for the steel mills directly and then indirectly when he worked for General Electric as an armature winder. He was always on call for emergencies to repair the huge industrial motors in the mills. Some were close to 100' around. He recollects baked bean sandwiches and corn meal mush day after day. They packed the leftover mush in a can or bread pan and chilled it until firm. It was then cut into thick pieces and fried in lard for another meal. My mother Adele Buck and I, are so very pleased to be able to participate in this cookbook commemorating steelworkers. We have submitted several recipes for your pleasure."

ADELE'S ITALIAN QUICHE

2 lb. sausage links	2 tbls. flour
1 onion, diced	2 cups grated Swiss cheese
8 Italian plum tomatoes,	2 tbls. grated Romano
peeled, seeded and chopped	1 cup cream or 1/2 cup milk
salt and pepper to taste	5 eggs, slightly beaten
pinch of basil, thyme and	unbaked pie crust (optional)
parsley	

Remove casing from sausage and crumble. Brown for 5 minutes and add onion. Continue cooking until onion is sauteed, then add tomatoes. Blend in spices and flour. Place sausage/tomato mixture and cheeses into pie crust or dish. (Mother did not use any crusts.) Combine cream and eggs. Pour over ingredients. Bake at 450° for 15 minutes then reduce oven to 375° and bake for 25 minutes or until done.

Adele Buck, Penn Hills

FETTUCCINI ALFREDO

1 box (12 oz.) fettuccini,
  cooked and drained
½ cup butter
½ cup heavy cream,
  room temperature

¾ cup Parmesan cheese
2 tbls. parsley
  salt and pepper

Toss well.

Shirley Kann, Monroeville

CHICKEN CACCIATORE

1 chicken, (2 ½ to 3 lb).cut up
½ cup flour
  salt and pepper
⅓ cup oil
1 medium onion
1 clove garlic, minced
½ cup sliced mushrooms
1 6 oz. can tomato paste

2 cups hot water
½ tsp. thyme
¼ tsp. oregano
¼ cup chopped parsley
¼ tsp. allspice
2 tsp. salt
¼ cup wine

Coat chicken with flour, salt and pepper and brown in oil. Add next three ingredients. In a sauce pan combine the next 7 ingredients and heat to boiling. Pour over chicken, cover and simmer for 45 minutes to 1 hour. Uncover and add wine. Makes 4 to 6 servings.

Shirley Kann, Monroeville

SHIRLEY'S ITALIAN BRISKET

4 lb. single brisket
1 envelope onion soup mix
¼ cup ketchup

¼ cup red wine
6 large potatoes, quartered and
  sprinkled with seasoned salt

Roast covered for 2 hours at 350°. Slice against grain, very thin.

Shirley Kann, Monroeville

ITALIANS

VEAL PARMESAN

1 lb. veal steak, thinly sliced	1/3 cup grated Parmesan cheese
salt and pepper	1/3 cup fine dry bread crumbs
1 egg	1/2 cup olive oil
2 tsps. water	

Cut veal into 6 to 8 pieces. Sprinkle with salt and pepper. Beat egg with water. Dip veal in egg, then roll in mixture of Parmesan cheese and bread crumbs. Heat oil in large skillet. Fry veal about 3 pieces at a time until golden brown on each side. Lay in shallow wide baking dish.

Sauce

2 tbls. olive oil	1 can (6 oz.) tomato paste
1/2 cup chopped onion	1 tsp. dried basil leaves
1 clove garlic, crushed	1 1/2 tsp. salt
1 can (2 lb. 3 oz.) Italian toma-	1/4 tsp. pepper
toes, undrained	1/2 lb. Mozzarella

In large skillet, saute first 3 ingredients until tender, about 5 minutes. Add tomatoes, tomato paste, salt and pepper. Bring to a boil, stirring with a wooden spoon. Reduce heat, simmer covered for 45 minutes stirring occasionally. Pour most of sauce over veal. Top with thin slices of cheese, then pour over remaining sauce. Baste in 350° moderate oven for about 30 minutes.

Rose Bikulege, Dormont

ZUCCHINI FRITTERS

1 cup flour	1 large egg
2 tsps. baking powder	1 medium size zucchini
3/4 tsp. salt	(or 2 cups)
1/2 cup grated Italian cheese	

Grate the zucchini before and let it drain. Zucchini has a lots of water in it.

Combine all ingredients and mix until moistened. Place a small amount of oil in a skillet. Drop batter in skillet to form small pancake. Fry until brown. Drain on paper towel.

Alice Manfredi, West Mifflin

DAD'S HOT OR COLD RATATOUILLE
ZUCCHINI AND EGGPLANT SALAD

1/3 cup olive oil	1 can plum tomatoes
3 cloves garlic, finely chopped	1 tsp. basil
2 large onions, sliced	1 1/2 tsps. salt
2 small eggplants, cubed	1 tsp. chopped parsley
4 small zucchini, sliced	fresh ground pepper
2 green peppers, cut in strips	

Heat oil and add garlic and onions. Saute until wilted, not brown. Add remaining ingredients and cover. Cook slowly for 1 hour, stirring occasionally. Uncover and cook 10 minutes more. Serve hot or cold with oil and vinegar on the side.

Pat Sommers, Munhall

SESAME SEED COOKIES

1 cup flour	1/4 tsp. salt
1 tsp. baking powder	1/4 cup sugar
1 whole egg	4 tbls. shortening
2 egg yolks	sesame seeds
1 tsp. vanilla	

Mix as for cake. Batter will be stiff. However, if it is too stiff, add a little milk. Roll in hand to thickness of hot dog, then cut in 1/2" pieces. Roll in seeds and bake in 375° oven for 10 minutes.

Adele Buck, Penn Hills

PIZZELLS
ITALIAN WAFFLE

4 cups flour	2 cups sugar
2 tsps. baking powder	1 cup vegetable oil
1 tsp. salt	1 tbl. vanilla or 1 tsp. anise
6 eggs	

Mix together first 3 ingredients and set aside. Beat eggs, sugar and oil. Add vanilla or anise. Add dry mixture and beat well. Pour 1/2 tsp. of mixture into center of hot pizzell iron. Makes 100 crispy pizzells.

Madelon Fazio, North Huntingdon

RICOTTA CAKE

2 lbs. ricotta	1 tsp. vanilla
¾ cup sugar	1 marble cake mix
3 large eggs	

Combine all ingredients except cake mix. Follow instructions on package for marble cake. After you have marbled it, add "lops" of ricotta mix on top of cake. Bake at 350° for 1 hour or more. Cool and ice.

Frosting

1 ½ cups cold milk	1 package chocolate instant
1 envelope whipped topping	pudding (4 serving size)
mix	

Pour milk into a deep narrow-bottom mixer bowl. Add whipped topping mix and pudding mix. Beat at low speed until well blended. Gradually increase beating speed to high and whip until soft peaks form, about 4 to 6 minutes.

Adele Buck, Penn Hills

NOODLE DESSERT

1 16 oz. can pineapple tidbits, reserve juice	1 tbl. lemon juice
	2 tbls. flour
2 small cans mandarin oranges, reserve juice	2 egg yolks, beaten
	1 box Romaria noodles, cooked and drained
¼ tsp. salt	
¾ cup sugar	1 large whipped topping

Place pineapple and mandarin orange juice in pan with salt, sugar, lemon juice and flour and bring to a boil. Slowly, by spoonfuls mix with egg yolks to bring them up to temperature, then add this to rest of mixture. Pour over noodles and fruit and cool. When cool, add whipped topping.

Ruth Ann Parkinson, West Mifflin

LOVE KNOTS
ITALIAN COOKIE

1 cup sugar

2 sticks margarine or butter

   (or 1 stick of each)

2 large eggs

½ cup evaporated milk

1 tsp. flavoring

   (anise, vanilla or lemon)

3-5 cups flour, as needed

4 ½ tsps. baking powder

Cream thoroughly sugar, butter or margarine, eggs and evaporated milk until light and fluffy. Add flavoring. Sift 3 cups flour with baking powder and add to creamed mixture. Remove dough to table and work in 1 ½ to 2 cups flour until dough is smooth. Do not add too much flour! Dough should be soft. Roll into rope-like strips about 1" around. Cut into 2" to 3" lengths and knot loosely. Place on a cookie sheet and bake at 350° for 8 to 10 minutes, until light brown on bottom. Do not overbake. Ice when cool. Confectioners sugar and warm water makes a light glaze. Also may be iced with butter frosting.

Rose Bikulege, Dormont

ITALIAN COOKIES

1 cup solid shortening

1 ¼ cups sugar

9 eggs

½ tsp. salt

3 ½ tbls. baking powder

2 ½ tbls. vanilla

7 cups flour

Cream shortening with sugar and eggs, one at a time. Beat until light. Add flavoring next three ingredients and mix well. Add flour. Place in refrigerator for 2 hours. Bake in 350° oven for 10 minutes.

Frosting

1 lb. confectioners sugar

   water

¼ tsp. cream of tartar

   food coloring

Adele Buck, Penn Hills

CHOCOLATE SPICE COOKIES

4 cups flour, sifted	3/4 cup cocoa, sifted
4 tsps. baking powder	1 1/2 cups sugar
1 tsp. salt	3/4 cup shortening
2 tsps. cinnamon	1 tsp. vanilla
1/2 tsp. nutmeg	1 1/2 cups chopped nuts
1/2 tsp. allspice	1 cup water

Mix together the first 8 ingredients. Then add shortening, vanilla and chopped nuts. Add just enough water to soften batter. Drop from spoon onto greased cookie sheet. Bake at 375° about 15 to 20 minutes. Makes about 5 dozen.

Betty Capalbo, West Mifflin

BISCOTTI
ITALIAN COOKIES

1/3 cup solid shortening	1/2 tsp. vanilla
1 cup sugar	3 drops anise extract
3 eggs	3 cups flour
1/2 tsp. salt	3 tsp. baking powder
1/2 tsp. almond extract	1/2 cup sliced almonds

Cream together the first 7 ingredients. Mix together the remaining ingredients, then add to cream mixture. Roll out 4 long rolls about 1 1/2" thick and 8" long. Put on a large cookie sheet. Bake at 325° until brown. Slice on an angle and toast in oven for about 5 minutes. Cookies should be a little hard and crunchy. Very good with wine or espresso coffee.

Alice Manfredi, West Mifflin

POLES

In the forty years before 1900, the Russian controlled section of Poland reeled under a 179 percent population growth, creating an over population of four to eight million people. Local jobs were impossible to come by, forcing Poles to look increasingly further abroad for employment. At first Poles worked in Brazil, Bosnia and the United States temporarily, returning to Poland with their earnings. The obsolescence of the household weaving trade, land monopolization and the czar's forced recruitment of young Poles sent a more permanent rush of immigrants to North America.

Starting in the early 1870s German Poles settled along Penn Avenue in the Strip District, followed by Russian Poles in Lawrenceville. Herron Hill, or Polish Hill, was inhabited by Poles from German held lands, who also settled on the South Side before 1900. After the turn of the century, Austrian Poles joined their compatriots in the South Side while Russian Poles sought friendship in Lawrenceville. By 1910 the Steel City was home to over 20,000 Polish immigrants.

Pittsburgh attracted family migration instead of individuals due to a great sense of kinship among Polish communities, according to John Bodnar in *Lives of Their Own: Blacks, Italians and Poles in Pittsburgh, 1900-1960*. Not only were immigrants ready to lend a hand once you arrived in town, but they would send detailed letters to Poland chock-full of practical information for newcomers.

Unlike Italians who were looking for social mobility, Poles wanted to find a steady income, leading to their reputation as hard workers, usually devoted to one company. In the Polish household, work and family life came before school and socializing. A 1973 survey by the city's Catholic diocese found over 60 percent of adults in a South Side Polish church had not graduated from high school, with a third having never gone beyond middle school.

POLISH COOKERY

Poland has a distinguished and distinctive cookery, which has evolved over the centuries because a talented people have concerned themselves seriously with their daily fare and still do. The word Pole is derived from Polani, the name of a tribe that lived between the Oder and Vistula rivers. Records of the Polani's organized settlement date from 966 AD. The Poles had to grow grains that could withstand a fierce northern climate, and fortunately their soil was well suited for cereal crops. Poland means "field country," and on its vast expanses the people grew rye, wheat, millet, barley and buckwheat groats. After the 18th century, when New World potatoes were introduced to Polish cookery, the potato, mixed with sour cream became the mainstay of the country table.

Cabbage in all its forms is one of the oldest traditional Polish foods. Soups are a particular Polish specialty, and one of the great favorites is Kapusniak, a fresh cabbage or sauerkraut dish enriched with marrow-bone, meat and dried mushrooms.

The Baltic Sea provided many types of seafood, but the Poles have long been particularly partial to eel and herring, which they eat fresh, salted, smoked, pickled or combined with other foods.

No food has been more highly regarded than the wide variety of wild mushrooms, which have appeared for centuries in abundance. In Poland, no Christmas Eve supper or other important meal would be complete without mushroom soup. Dried Polish mushrooms, exported to Western Europe and America, are sought-after delicacies.

Another precious forest food was honey, and beekeeping early became an important occupation. Many kinds of honey were used extensively in cookery, and Polish honey cakes and cookies were destined to become world famous.

For meats, the Poles relied heavily on the superb game and wild birds found in the forests. Hunting was a national pastime and the cooking of duck, venison, pheasant etc. was an accomplished art. The wild pig, when domesticated and pampered in backyards or farms, became an important food. Even today Polish hams and sausages (kielbasi) are rated among the world's best.

NATIONAL SPICE

All members of the onion family. Dill was the essential herb. Nuts and poppy seeds also came to be widely used, and in later years, spices introduced from the East, such as cinnamon, nutmeg, pepper, cloves and saffron, became symbols of wealth for those who could afford them.

Poles also relied on such foods as anchovies, capers, lemon and horseradish to achieve the piquant flavorings preferred by the Slavs.

POLISH CUSTOMS

The Hyacinth is the traditional Polish Easter Flower.

Easter Monday is a Holiday in Poland. An old tradition, Smigus or Dyngus, consists of a splash of cold water waiting for them at every city corner or even a sprinkle in their own bed on Easter Monday.

Polish tradition requires one to invite to the Christmas Eve Dinner not only the people one likes, but primarily those who are lonely, unhappy or sick. It used to be the only meal of the year shared by the servants with their Master and his family at the same table.

Hospitality was always considered sacred in Poland. No harm could come to a guest because Poles believed that "A guest in the house — is God in the House."

Among the Poles, the most beloved and beautiful of all their traditional festivities is that of Christmas Eve. The Wilia Supper is served on Christmas Eve when the first star appears in the Eastern sky. The Supper itself differs from other evening meals in that the number of courses is fixed at seven, nine or eleven; and in no case must there be an odd number of people at the table. Fish is the basic food in the many-course Wilia Supper.

POLSKE PACZKI

1 cake yeast	1/2 cup sugar
1 pt. milk, scalded and cooled	1/2 tsp. vanilla
6-7 cups all purpose flour, divided	1 grated lemon rind
	1 tsp. salt
1 whole egg	1 stick butter, melted
4 egg yolks	

Dissolve yeast in lukewarm milk and add 2 cups flour. Allow to stand in a warm place for 1/2 hour. Beat next 6 ingredients together until mixture is very light (at least 10 minutes with an electric mixer at high speed). Add yeast-flour mixture. Add melted butter and remaining flour. (This is usually 4 to 5 cups). Mix until smooth. Cover and allow to double in bulk in a warm place.

Turn out dough on a lightly floured board and roll out to 1/2" thickness. Cut with a doughnut cutter or glass for filled doughnuts. I use a large water glass. Put on cookie sheets. Cover and let rise again until double in bulk and light. Preheat fat or shortening to 365°. Use sufficient fat to cover the doughnuts. Slip enough doughnuts into hot fat so that they will not be crowded and fry to a golden brown on both sides. Drain well.

To fill: Make a slit about 1 1/2" long on the side. Use any favorite preserves (strawberry, raspberry, apricot, and prune for the fillings. Using a teaspoonful of preserves, push into the doughnut, leaving the preserves inside. Pull closed and roll in sugar. Eating them warm is wonderful!

Elaine Jaworski

"Twenty-five years ago, as the mother of three small children, I wanted them to grow up familiar with some traditions from their Polish heritage. Among those traditions was our celebration of Paczki Day.
Paczki Day, also known as Shrove Tuesday, is the day before Ash Wednesday, the first day of the Catholic Lenten season. Paczki, homemade jelly-filled doughnuts, provided a final sweet treat before the fasting and penance of Lent.
What began as a simple family celebration grew over the years to include as many as 50 people. Preparations would begin in the early afternoon ,and we made as many as 21 dozen paczki. Friends gathered at our home to enjoy the doughnuts, coffee and friendship. The gathering always included children, who enjoyed the treat the most. Now that my children have grown and moved out of state, I continue this on a smaller scale. My daughter also carries on this tradition and has introduced it to her friends in Atlanta, Georgia."

BIALY BARSZCZ
WHITE BORSCHT

2 qts. water	½ bay leaf
1 cup diced boiled ham	¾ cup sour cream
½ lb. smoked kielbasa	2 tsps. sifted flour
2 tsps. salt	sour salt
5 peppercorns (whole pepper)	marjoram (optional)
2 buds garlic	sliced hard-boiled eggs

Bring the water to a boil. Skin and thinly slice the kielbasa (Polish sausage). Add the ham, kielbasa, salt, peppercorns, garlic and bay leaf. Cook at a gentle boil for 30 to 40 minutes.

Using a fork, blend the sour cream and flour. Add the hot soup stock at the rate 1 tsp. at a time, stirring constantly, until you have about 2 cups of the mixture. Remove the soup stock from the heat and slowly add the sour cream and flour mixture.

If you do not have sour salt, use citric acid crystals or a concentrated citrus juice to make the soup tart to the taste. Add a pinch of marjoram, if you wish. The soup may be served over slices of hard-boiled eggs. The amount of egg is up to your taste, but a couple of slices will ordinarily suffice. This dish is traditionally served at Easter.

ZUPA JABTKOWA
APPLE SOUP

6 large apples	½ cup lemon juice
1 qt. water	1 cup whipping cream
¾ cup sugar	⅔ cup white wine (optional)
½ tsp. cinnamon	

Pare and core 5 apples. Cook in water until soft. Rub through a sieve or puree in blender to make an apple sauce. Combine applesauce, sugar and cinnamon in a large bowl. Shred or mince remaining apple and mix with lemon juice. Stir into applesauce mixture. Chill. To serve, blend cream into applesauce mixture. Stir in wine. If desired, you may substitute 16 oz. jar or can of applesauce and one cup of water for the 5 apples and water.

Sophie Lizik

TOK LASKA
PUMPKIN SOUP

1 small pumpkin (green prefer-ably, but not necessary)	3 tbls. flour
1 tbl. salt	1 small onion (finely diced)
2 qts. water	1 tbl. butter
1 tsp salt	1 cup chicken broth (hot) or
1/4 tsp. pepper	1 cup tomato juice instead of
1 pint sour cream	the broth

Shred pumpkin. Sprinkle with 1 tablespoon salt and let sit. Bring water with salt and pepper to a boil. Squeeze pumpkin well to make it as dry as possible. Then drop pumpkin in boiling water and bring to a boil again. Saute butter and onion until onion is soft and clear and add to the pumpkin mixture. Slowly add blended sour cream and flour to the chicken broth and add to the pumpkin mixture. Heat but do not boil. Pumpkin mixture may be processed in a food processor or blender until smooth before adding the chicken broth and sour cream if you prefer a smoother texture. May use sour cream lite if desired. However, butter is essential for taste. Season to taste and serve.

Stephanie Paul, Baldwin

SZCZUPAK P POLSKU
NORTHERN PIKE POLISH STYLE

1 northern pike	10 peppercorns
4 cups water	2 1/2 tbls. lemon juice
1 carrot	salt and pepper
1 onion	10 eggs
1 stalk celery	2 tbls. butter

Add to water in a pan the carrot, onion, celery stalk, peppercorns and 1/2 tablespoon lemon juice. Salt well. Put the cleaned fish into the pan and boil for 30 minutes. Meanwhile boil the eggs and chop them well. Heat 2 tablespoons of butter in a skillet, add chopped eggs and 2 tablespoons of lemon juice. Salt and pepper to taste. When fish is cooked, take it from saucepan and pour egg sauce over the top.

BIGOS
HUNTER'S STEW

6 lbs. diced cooked meat (use at least ½ lb. each of the following: beef, ham, lamb, sausage, veal, pork, venison or rabbit, wild duck, wild goose or pheasant)	2 tbls. flour
	1 pound fresh mushrooms, sliced or three 4 oz. cans sliced undrained
	1 - 2 cups water or bouillon
5 ozs. salt pork, diced	6 lbs. sauerkraut
1 onion, minced	2 tsps. pepper
2 leeks, minced	2 tsps. sugar
	1 cup Madeira

Fry salt pork until golden but not crisp in an 8 quart kettle. Add onion and leeks. Stir-fry for 3 minutes. Stir in flour. Add mushrooms with liquid and water to kettle. Simmer 5 minutes. Drain and rinse sauerkraut. Add to kettle along with cooked meat, salt, pepper and sugar. Cover, cook over medium to low heat for 1 ½ hours. Stir in wine. Add more salt, pepper, and sugar to taste. Simmer 15 minutes. Do not boil. Serves 12-16.

Sophie Lizik

If meat must be prepared especially for this stew, each piece should be braised separately. Put meat, poultry or game into Dutch oven with one carrot, one stalk celery, one onion, one parsnip, one clove garlic or one sprig parsley, five peppercorns, one cup water and one cup wine. Simmer covered until meat is tender. When wine is added, chopped apples, heavy cream, and/or cooked small potatoes may also be added.
This most delectable dish was served at every hunting party.
It is Poland's National Dish and is also known as Shepherd's Soup.

KONSERWOWANE BRZOSKWINIE
BRANDIED PEACHES

1 peck peaches, skinned	1 qt. brandy
sugar to half their weight	

Alternate in stone jar, layers of peaches with sugar until filled. Add brandy. Cover closely, using cheesecloth or unbleached muslin under the jar cover. Ready to use after one week. Keep in cool place.

ALMAS LEPENG
APPLE SQUARES

Dough

3	cups all purpose flour	3	tsps. baking powder
2	sticks butter or ½ lb.	1	lemon,
3	egg yolks		juice and rind only
½	cup granulated sugar	¾	cup sour cream

Filling

¼	cup soda cracker crumbs	1 ½	tsps. grated lemon rind
5	apples sliced	½	cup ground or chopped nuts

Prepare butter and flour as for pie dough. Add rest of ingredients. Pat ½ of the dough into a greased 13" x 9" pan. Mix filling and spread gently over the dough. Sprinkle with a little cinnamon sugar. Pat rest of dough on top of apple filling. Sprinkle with nuts and a little more cinnamon sugar. Bake 325° until light brown.

Stephanie Paul, Baldwin

HOT SQUASH BREAD

3	cups thinly sliced unpeeled zucchini (any squash may be substituted, yellow, butternut, etc.)	1 ½	tsp. garlic salt or
		1	clove garlic, finely chopped
		1	tsp. chopped parsley
		1	small onion, chopped
1	cup bisquick	½	cup oil
4	eggs, well beaten	½	cup parmesan cheese

Grease 8"x 8" square pan. Mix all ingredients together. Bake for 35 minutes at 350°. Serve warm.

Stephanie Paul, Baldwin

JEWS

It wasn't until the late 1840s that German Jews made their way to Pittsburgh, coinciding with the emergence of the city as a link to the west. The early Jews came from Bavaria, Baden and Wurtemberg, with a smaller group arriving from Poland and Russia, all hoping to find prosperity in the Steel City's rapidly expanding economy.

Jews arrived through the 1930s, with the Eastern European and German groups forming separate communities in the city. The first Jews lived in the downtown area around Market Street while the German Jews moved north to Allegheny City. The Rodef Shalom, representing the Reform views of the German Jews, was established in 1854 while the Etz Chaim or Tree of Life began services for the more Orthodox Poles, Dutch and Lithuanian Jews a decade later.

By the 1860s most of the city's major retail and wholesale food stores were owned by Jews, while others worked as merchants, traders, tailors, mechanics and peddlers. A few of the wealthier families invested in the iron and steel industries. A stereotype that Jews could not perform manual labor kept many from being hired into the mills, even by Jewish mill owners. Many Jews took to peddling, teaching newcomers the ways of the city quickly. A good number of these men eventually owned their own businesses, cigar production being a popular endeavor in the 1880s.

The size of the area's Jewish community doubled between 1880 and 1887 due to the influx of a thousand Lithuanian Jews, followed in the 1880s by Rumanian, Polish, Hungarian and Russian Jews. Political and economic pressure, combined with religious oppression, had started a vast migration of Jews from their Eastern European homelands. By 1917 there were 40,000 Jews in Pittsburgh.

As the numbers expanded Jews moved from downtown to the Hill District and later, between the world wars, to Oakland and Squirrel Hill, establishing synagogues, schools and cohesive communities.

WHITEFISH APPETIZER

1 egg	1 tbl. chives, minced
3 tbls. sour cream	salt to taste
1 1/2 tbls. mayonnaise	1 1/2 lbs. ocean whitefish, cooked
2 tsps. prepared mustard	(sole may be substituted)
1 tbl. parsley, minced	

Beat the egg lightly and stir in the sour cream, mayonnaise, mustard, parsley and chives. Add salt to taste. Pour over the fish, toss lightly and spoon into 6 individual shell-shaped baking dishes. Bake in a pre-heated, 400° oven for 12 to 15 minutes.

GEFILTE FISH
RUSSIAN STYLE

This dish would be appropriate for a Passover Seder.

6 lbs. carp or pike, ground	salt and pepper to taste
salt	1 lb. carrots, thinly sliced
1 lb. onions, finely chopped	3 lbs. beets, thinly sliced
3 egg yolks, beaten	4 large Spanish onions,
3 egg whites, whipped	thinly sliced
1/2 cup matzo meal	cold water to cover
2 tbls. oil	

Cut whole fish into 2" slices. Carefully remove flesh without breaking skin and bones. Salt the skins and bones and place in bowl while preparing filling. Grind or process the flesh to a coarse consistency, like ground meat. Mix together ground fish and onions. Add eggs (yolks and whites), matzo meal, oil and salt and pepper. Mix thoroughly. Wet hands with cold water. Form oval fish patties and fit them into the fish skins.

Place head and any other bones in the bottom of a deep heavy pot. Add enough carrots, beets and onions to cover bottom of pot. Lay wrapped patties on top of vegetables. Separate each patty with a sliced beet. Keep alternating vegetable layers with fish patty layers. Add cold water seasoned with salt and pepper to to cover. Cover pan and bring to a quick boil. Reduce heat and simmer 1 1/2 hours covered. Cook 1 more hour without lid. Cool. Carefully remove patties and place on a platter. Garnish with cooked vegetables. Refrigerate. Serve with horse-radish. Makes 8 to 10 servings.

CARROT TSIMES AND KNADEL

Tsimes

1/2 lb.brisket of beef	2 cups water
1 onion, small	2 lbs. carrots, diced
1 t.salt	1/2 cup sugar

Put brisket, onion and salt in water. Bring to a boil. Lower heat, cover and simmer for 1 hour. Add the carrots and sugar. Cook until carrots are tender, about 20 to 30 minutes.

Knadel

2 med. potatoes, grated	1 tbl. onion, grated
1 tbl. matzo meal	1/2 tsp. salt
1 1/2 tbl. chicken broth	1/4 tsp. black pepper

Drain the grated potatoes. Remove excess moisture by draining thoroughly. Add rest of ingredients and spread over the top of the tsimes. Place in baking dish and bake at 350° for about 20 minutes until slightly browned. Serves 6.

ORANGE AND LEMON KEZEL

1 large orange	2/3 cup sugar
1 large lemon	4 tbl. matzo meal
4 eggs	1/2 cup chopped nuts, optional

Bring fruit (left whole) to a boil in water. Pour off water and refill pan with water. Bring to another boil and pour off water again. Add fresh water a third time and boil until fruit is tender. Drain. Open fruit and allow to cool. Remove seeds. Mash fruit and pulp. Set aside. Beat the eggs, sugar and matzo meal until foamy. Add fruit pulp. Add nuts, if desired. Bake 50 minutes at 325°.

1990 demolition of Homestead Works, Open Hearth No. 5. Photo courtesy Randolph Harris.

Erected in 1941 by the Defense Plant Corporation, OH5 was the last open hearth furnace built by U.S. Steel in this area.

POST WORLD WAR II

The renowned manufacturing Goliath of Pittsburgh heroically emerged from the smoke of World War II to find itself still in the smoke, with severe pollution, overcrowding and flood control problems. Karl Schriftgiesser describes the Steel City to his *Atlantic Monthly* readers in 1951: "The decrepitude showed in its worn out office buildings, its degraded housing, its traffic-choked streets, its sordid alleys, its polluted and uncontrolled rivers, and, above all, in the dense choking smoke that covered the city and the river valleys..."

Suddenly "Smoke Must Go!" signs began appearing on trolleys — Pittsburgh's renaissance was under way. The construction of civic buildings, strict smoke control laws, and an immense clean-up effort marked such a change in the city, it would be decades before the rest of the country would get over its incredulity.

As Pittsburgh was repositioning itself as one of the nation's most attractive places to live, the steel industry's foundations were crumbling. Historians point to the 116 day strike in 1959 — when 500,000 USW workers nationwide, 150,000 in Pittsburgh, walked off the job — as the beginning of the steel empire's deterioration. Some historians point to the long-standing animosity between labor, management and government as the reason foreigners were able to grab large shares of the business.

Others contend employee ownership incentives or government artificially inflating the need for steel might have saved the industry debacle that wrecked whole towns in western Pennsylvania. Still others blame investment in foreign steelmaking or the decision not to upgrade equipment as the culprit. "It was pretty obvious to anyone coming to Homestead in the late 70s and looking at the quality of equipment, or going to Youngstown and seeing steam engines still powering rolling mills, that something was drastically wrong," said Charles McCollester in a paper presented to the Western Pennsylvania Historical Society in 1990.

The 1960s saw a 20 percent decline in manufacturing jobs from the 150,000 available the previous decade. Fifty-five thousand jobs were lost in the 1970s and by the early 1980s the crucible had collapsed, eliminating nearly 100,000 weekly paychecks. Mill activity in 1989 only called for 20,000 laborers, down from 120,000 four decades before.

While the call of the steel industry once drew people from as far off as Byelorussia, Italy and Bulgaria, the mills' silence now generated flight to other jobs and other places. Some people left — the oil fields of Texas being a popular destination, some moved to suburbs like Monroeville and Penn Hills to seek work, others went for retraining or back to school or started their own businesses. Once the Steel Capital of the World, producing 40 percent of the total nation's production, Pittsburgh has gone through one more Renaissance than it counted on. But because it was one of the biggest in the industry, it was one of the first to fall. Since the late 1970s steel production has severely decreased in Germany, France, Luxembourg and the fall of the Soviet Empire has brought metal manufacturing in Eastern Europe nearly to a standstill.

Though the industry that brought immigrants here is all but dissolved, the people and where they worked plays too large a role in the development of the region to be forgotten. The Steel Industry Heritage Corporation is planning a 75-acre heritage center to preserve, exhibit and explain the steel mills and their singular cultural heritage to visitors. The Carrie Furnace in Rankin and Swissvale, Homestead's Bost Building, and the Pinkerton Landing in Munhall are among the sites and artifacts to be preserved.

THE LUNCH PAIL

What do you eat when you work in the mill where there is no refrigeration or a place to cook? You have to work a twelve hour day, and you just have to have something to eat.

In the early days of the mill, processed foods would take the form of cheese, sausages and other natural foods that were either smoked, pickled, salted or cured in some way as to make them palatable for extended periods of time. The only other choices were fresh foods that spoiled easily.

During the lunch periods young children would carry their fathers lunches in galvanized steel pails covered by embroidered cloths or flat steel lids into the mills. Older children ages 12 and up were employed as water boys, responsible for making sure there was always enough water for the "hot" jobs and during lunch.

The various ethnic groups had differences in their lunch pail diet based upon the origins of their diet. For example: the Blacks had a diet of fresh greens, corn bread and other foods from their ethnic menu. The Slavs, Slovaks, Russians, Ukrainians and Bulgarians usually had cheese,

City Farm Lane Gate near the "Hole in the Wall" and east parking lot stairs.

sausages and rye bread as the mainstay of their diet. Certain foods were held in common by all the groups such as hard boiled eggs and water or in the early days beer or wine.

One steelworker, Dan Karaczun, relates that during the latter stages of the mills history the tradition of the 4 to 12 shift dinner became known to him. On more than one occasion he would participate in the planned dinner that usually took place on the last day of the shift.

Someone would ask all the people on the shift if they were interested in participating in the dinner. Those who were interested would indicate that they were and the planning began.

It was the sole responsibility of the instigator and perhaps a friend to buy all the ingredients, cook the meal and clean up afterwards.

During the 4 to 12 shift at the Structural Soaking Pits as a Metallurgical Observer, Dan and his best friend Alex, a Soaking Pit Recorder, decided that they would offer a dinner of Chinese Pepper Steak to the entire Pit crew; the Foreman, Heater, Pit Cranemen, Pit Recorders and Laborers. Most of the men decided that they were in, somewhere around fourteen men as Dan recalls. He and his wife carefully calculated the amounts of beef, peppers, onions, rice, garlic, black pepper salt, oil and soy sauce needed for fourteen men. During the early part of the day they shopped for the needed ingredients and supplied what else was needed from their cupboard. He carried two shopping bags of food into the mill that day from the main gate to his locker room at Open Hearth No. 5, changed into work clothes and carried the bags about a mile to the Structural Soaking Pits.

Dan and Alex began cooking the meal about 6:30 while attempting to dispose of their work responsibilities at the same time. One hour later the smells of the Pepper Steak filled the pit office as they began to serve the meal. Several of the men came back for seconds and the meal was judged to be a tremendous success. After the clean up which took a half hour, they began to catch up on their work at about 8:30. They calculated the contribution of each man who ate and the money was collected to repay them for what had been spent. The electric fry pans were returned to the men who contributed them, the tea that remained was poured out into the sink and everyone left the mill that night with the anticipation of twenty-four hours off until they began the 12 to 8, or graveyard shift.

Many meals like this one were prepared by others at the Structural Soaking Pits. Matt, one of the heaters prepared his famous chili once. Another time it was liver and onions with home fried potatoes. Sometimes someone would bring in meatball hoagies or hot sausage sandwiches from a local Italian restaurant in his neighborhood. Everyone ate well during the 4 to 12 shift when the superintendents were no longer around and the foremen became just one of the working men and not just representatives of management. When the big bosses were gone, men would bring in leftovers from the previous days home dinner from which they were absent and take care in the re-heating on the home made hot plates made by the motor inspectors and electricians in the shops around the mill.

Night turn was the worst! No one really felt like eating. When you did eat a lot, you got a slightly sick feeling for the rest of the shift. No large dinners on 12 to 8. Some inventive people in Metallurgical Observation over at Open Hearth No. 5 would cook a breakfast of bacon and eggs at about 5:00 on the last shift of night turn. But mostly, people ate because they had to eat something and not because they expected to enjoy it.

Wherever there is heat, next to a furnace or one of the home made hot plates, you could always find someone heating leftovers. Even sandwiches tasted better hot than they did cold. Ham and cheese became toasted ham and melted cheese. The problem with heating food next to a furnace was that you had to have the time and opportunity to pay attention to your job and your lunch. One time Dan placed a Mason jar next to 71 furnace in OH-5. A string of charging buggies was placed in front of the furnace to charge the next heat and he was blocked out from the food. By the time he got to the jar, the food on one side was burnt and the other side was still frozen due to the winter cold. The only heat radiated by the furnace was within a few inches of the refractory bricks. Needless to say, Dan had no lunch that night.

Daylight on the 8 to 4 turn had no such inventions as the 4 to 12 or 12 to 8 turns. The eyes of management were everywhere and convoluted preparations of food were discouraged. So, most steel workers ate sandwiches of some sort. Anything that had to be heated or prepared in any way was discouraged if not forbidden outright. The supervisors had this sacrificial attitude about making steel even though they had a cafeteria with carefully prepared hot meals for $25 a month. For the men who had not taken sandwiches, the canteen would sell hot sandwiches, chili, soups and a hot meal for about three to four dollars a meal. The problem was to find the time to walk to the canteen, wait in line to order, eat the meal and walk back to the shop, all in about twenty minutes. Quite a contrast to what management ate and paid. Everywhere in the mill the feeling was that what was purchased in the canteen subsidized the management meals in the General Office Building Cafeteria. Whether it was true or not is relatively unimportant because the perception was that the workers paid for the lunches of the bosses.

No matter what people ate in the mills, the job was always a job well done. The inventiveness that men and women used to prepare food at work was also used in keeping aged machinery productive. Worn or broken parts were used with the experienced eyes of craftsmen and artists to continue to produce quality steel in abundance.

SPAGHETTI OMELET
GOOD MANAGEMENT

1. Set oven at 375°; spread 8 slices of bacon (about ½ lb.) in a shallow pan, and put in to bake while you do the omelet. (Bacon will bake crisp in 10 to 15 minutes; does not have to be turned.)
2. Drain canned peach halves; arrange them on lettuce, and fill with mayonnaise or French dressing blended with sweet pickle relish.
3. Arrange big plate with small dish of strawberry or raspberry jam in center, mound of cheese next to dish, crackers around edge.

2 tbls. bacon drippings,	1 can spaghetti with tomato
butter or margarine	sauce (about 1 lb.)
3 eggs, separated	½ lb. bacon
½ tsp. salt	(bake as in No. 1 above)
¼ tsp. pepper	

Heat oven 375°. Heat drippings in large, heavy skillet with removable or heat-resistant handle. Beat egg yolks with fork; stir in salt, pepper, and spaghetti. Beat egg whites stiff and fold into spaghetti mixture. Pour mixture into skillet, spreading it evenly. Cook (without stirring) over medium heat, until underside of omelet is firm and lightly browned. Transfer skillet and contents to 375° oven; bake 10 minutes or until surface feels firm when touched with finger. Fold over; serve immediately with crisp bacon. Makes 4 servings.

The Daily Messenger, February 25, 1950

BABY BURGERS

½ lb. chuck or round-beef	¼ tsp. salt
ground	⅛ tsp. pepper
1 egg	⅛ tsp. onion salt
2 tbls. minced green pepper	15 saltines

Preheat broiler 10 minutes or as manufacturer directs. Combine ground beef and next 5 ingredients and mix thoroughly. Spread on saltines, completely covering each. Broil 2 minutes or until brown. Serve immediately, with tossed salad or hot soup, or as an appetizer. Makes 5 servings.

The Daily Messenger, February 24, 1950

In making lemonade strain the juice, and to improve the taste allow a half dozen oranges to every dozen lemons. If desired a few thin rounds of banana may be added.
Homestead Local News, December 15, 1892

OYSTER LOAF

1/4 lb. butter or margarine	1 loaf unsliced enriched white bread (about 1 lb. 1 oz.)

About half an hour ahead of time, take out butter to soften. When butter is spreadable, turn on oven, set at 350°. Cut about 1/3"off top of bread. Then, with fork, remove most of crumbs from loaf, leaving shell about 1" thick. Spread butter on inside of shell and on inside of top crust. Place in shallow pan and set aside.

1 qt. fresh or thawed frozen medium oysters (24 to 32)	2 tsps. salt
3 tbls. butter or margarine	1/4 tsp. pepper
	2 tbls. minced parsley or chives

Drain oysters, reserving 1/3 cup liquid. Heat butter in skillet. Drop in oysters; then cook over medium heat 3 minutes or until barely heated, occasionally stirring and sprinkling with salt and pepper. Add reserved 1/3 cup liquid; heat 1 minute longer. Stir in parsley. Pour oysters into prepared bread loaf; put on top crust. Carefully slash through top crust part way, marking off 4 to 6 slices. (Slicing will be easier at serving time.) Bake at 350° 15 to 20 minutes — it should be lightly crisped outside, heated through.

lemon or lime wedges	chili sauce, catchup, or cheese or tomato sauce

When oyster loaf is baked, transfer it to heated platter and garnish with lemon or line wedges. At table "carve" loaf into slices using markings as guides. Serve with chili sauce or other flavorsome sauce. Makes 4 to 6 servings — a contrast of crunchy top crust and juice-laden bottom crust with plump, succulent oysters inside. How to eat it? Guests use their fingers for the toasty bread and attack the oysters with a fork.

The Daily Messenger, February 23, 1950

Sandwiches can be made some hours before needed if kept in a cool place snugly covered with a damp cloth. They should be piled closely upon a dish.
Homestead Local News, December 14, 1893

THREE-IN-ONE BEEF PIE

¾ lb. boneless chuck or round beef, cut in 3/4" cubes

2 tbls. flour

1 tsp. salt

¼ tsp. pepper

2 tbls. bacon drippings

1 ½ cups boiling water

2 tsps. Worcestershire sauce

⅓ tsp. bottled thick meat sauce

¼ tsp. garlic salt

½ cup sliced onion

1 cup pared, diced potatoes (1 medium)

1 thinly sliced, pared carrot

¾ cup drained canned or thawed frozen peas

⅓ pkg. piecrust mix

water

Night before:

Trim fat and gristle from meat. Mix next three ingredients on plate. Roll meat in flour mixture to coat well on all sides. Reserve leftover flour, if any. Heat bacon drippings in saucepan; add floured meat, and brown thoroughly on all sides. Add leftover flour, boiling water, Worcestershire, bottled meat sauce, and garlic salt. Stir until blended. Cover tightly; cook slowly until tender — about 1 hour. Add onion, potatoes, carrot. Cook covered about 10 minutes or until vegetables are tender but still crisp. Chill until needed next night.

Next night:

Place your top-stove oven over medium-high heat. Remove chilled meat and vegetables from refrigerator; reheat. Meanwhile, make top crust, using ⅓ pkg. piecrust mix and water as directed on package. When meat mixture is hot, add peas; pour into 1 qt. casserole. Prick top crust with fork, and arrange on top of casserole. Trim to fit casserole, then press tightly to it. When heat indicator on top-stove oven points to 4 (about 400°) place meat pie in oven. Bake 20 to 30 minutes or until golden brown on top. Makes 2 generous servings.

The Daily Messenger, February 25, 1950.

Tea and coffee often leave a brown rim around the bottom of cups and saucers. This discoloration can be removed by scouring with salt that has been a little dampened.
Homestead Local News, January 31, 1894

BAKED SEA-FOOD SALAD

1 cup cleaned fresh shrimp, canned or cooked	1 cup mayonnaise
1 cup fresh crab meat, canned or cooked	1 tsp. Worcestershire sauce
1/2-3/4 cup green pepper, chopped, seeded	1/2 tsp. salt
1/4 cup minced onion	1/4 tsp. pepper
1 cup thinly sliced celery	1/2 cup soft bread crumbs
	1 tbl. butter or margarine, melted

Early in day, cut shrimp in halves crosswise; flake crab meat. Combine and add green pepper, onion, celery, mayonnaise, Worcestershire, salt and pepper; mix lightly. Spread in 10" x 6" x 2" baking dish.

Toss bread crumbs with melted butter; sprinkle over mixture. Refrigerate until about 40 minutes before dinner. Bake in 300° oven 30 to 40 minutes or until nicely browned. Serve with sprigs of parsley and lemon quarters. Makes 4 generous servings.

If salad is prepared and baked immediately, bake at 350° 30 minutes.

The Daily Messenger, January 27, 1950

APPLE QUICKEE

2 cups graham-cracker crumbs, rolled fine (about 28)	1/2 tsp. cinnamon
3 tbls. butter or margarine	1/4 cup chopped walnuts
1 No. 2 can applesauce	1/2 cup heavy cream

Combine cracker crumbs and butter; mix until crumbly. Mix applesauce, cinnamon, and nuts thoroughly. Arrange 4 layers crumbs and 3 layers applesauce in 9" x 5" x 3" loaf pan, beginning and ending with crumb layer. Chill thoroughly. Serve with sweetened whipped cream. Makes 4 to 5 servings.

The Daily Messenger, February 24, 1950

CHOCOLATE-GRAHAM PUDDING

1 ¼ cups graham-cracker crumbs,
rolled fine (about 20)

¼ tsp. salt

⅓ cup brown sugar,
firmly packed

1 cup milk

2 egg yolks, beaten

¼ cup butter or margarine

1 cup semi-sweet chocolate
pieces

2 egg whites, beaten stiff

Heat oven to 325°. Combine crumbs and next 4 ingredients. Melt butter and chocolate together over hot water. Add to cracker mixture. Fold in egg whites. Pour into 6 greased custard cups. Bake at 325° 45 minutes or until cake tester inserted in center comes out clean. Serve warm with cream or ice cream. Makes 6 servings.

The Daily Messenger, February 24, 1950

BAZLAMACA
CORNBREAD
CROATIAN

16 ozs. cottage cheese

½ cup granulated sugar

2 eggs

½ tsp. salt

½ stick margarine, melted

½ cup yellow cornmeal

½ cup flour

¼ tsp. baking soda

½ pint sour cream

1 cup milk

Mix first 4 ingredients. Add remaining ingredients, mix well. Place in a greased 9" x 9" pan. Bake in 425° oven until top is nice and brown, about 1 hour and 15 minutes. You can add ½ cup of raisins.

Helen Lazaro, Pittsburgh

If you have cream you want to keep sweet a few days, add two or three lumps of sugar, stirring it well, then cover it and set it away in the coldest corner of the refrigerator.
Pittsburgh Courier, 1912

KISELO ZELJE PASULJ JUHA
SAUERKRAUT AND BEAN SOUP
CROATIAN

1 small onion	1 large can sauerkraut
1 lb. kolbassi	3 tbls. oil
1 lb. can kidney beans, drained	4 tbls. flour

Cook kolbassi for 20 minutes in a 6 quart pot ½ with water. In the meantime, wash sauerkraut slightly. Add to kolbassi and cook another 10 to 15 minutes. To this add kidney beans and continue to cook over low heat about 1 ½ hours.

Helen Lazaro, Pittsburgh

YORKSHIRE PUDDING
ENGLISH

⅞ cup flour	2 eggs
½ tsp. salt	½ cup water
½ cup milk	

Preheat oven to 400°.

Ingredients must be at room temperature when mixed or they will not puff. Sift together flour and salt into a bowl. Make a well in the center, and pour in milk. Stir.

Beat eggs until fluffy and add to the batter. Add water.

Beat batter well until large bubbles rise to surface. You may permit this to stand covered and refrigerated for 1 hour and then beat again. Have ready a hot oven-proof dish about 9" x 12", or hot muffin tins containing about ¼" hot beef drippings, such as the juices from standing rib roast, or melted butter. Pour in batter. It should be about ⅝" high.

Bake pudding for about 20 minutes. Reduce heat to 350° and bake it 10 to 15 minutes longer. Serve at once. Serves 6.

PEANUT BUTTER FUDGE
ENGLISH

2 cups sugar

½ cup milk

6 tbls. margarine

1 7 oz. jar marshmallow creme

1 12 oz. jar peanut butter

Combine sugar, milk and margarine and cook to medium hard boil. Add marshmallow creme and peanut butter. Beat and pour in buttered pan.

Dolores M. Zewe, Duquesne

CLOVE CRESCENTS
GREEK

Basic Dough

1 ½ cups butter or margarine, softened

1 ½ cups confectioners sugar

1 egg

1 tsp. vanilla

2 ½ cups flour

Preheat oven to 375°. Mix first 4 ingredients thoroughly. Blend in four. Divide dough in half.

½ tsp. brandy flavoring

whole cloves

To one half Basic Dough recipe, mix in brandy flavoring. Shape dough by rounded teaspoonfuls into balls and crescents. Press whole clove into center of each. Bake on ungreased baking sheet 10 to 12 minutes or until set but not brown. Cool; dust with confectioners sugar.

Makes about 3 dozen per half Basic Dough.

MEXICAN SQUASH
MEXICAN

1 clove garlic, minced
2 cups summer squash, sliced
2 cups zucchini, sliced
1/2 cup dry bread crumbs
1/2 cup freshly grated Parmesan
  cheese
1/2 cup milk
1 tbl. minced fresh parsley
1/2 tsp. salt

1/8 tsp. ground black pepper
1/2 tsp. dried oregano, crushed
2 4 oz. cans diced green chilies
1/2 cup shredded Cheddar cheese
2 eggs, beaten
1/2 cup soft bread crumbs
1/2 cup butter, melted
1/2 cup shredded Cheddar cheese

In large covered saucepan, cook garlic, squash and zucchini in small amount of water until tender, drain.

Stir dry bread crumbs, Parmesan cheese, milk, parsley, salt, pepper, oregano, green chilies and 1/2 cup Cheddar cheese into vegetables. Fold in beaten eggs.

Pour mixture into a 6" x 10" baking dish. Toss soft bread crumbs with melted butter. Sprinkle casserole with buttered bread crumbs and 1/2 cup Cheddar cheese. Bake at 325° for 25 to 30 minutes. Serves 6.

Irene Parkinson, West Mifflin

HARD-BOILED EGGS WITH SAUSAGE
SPANISH

6 eggs

2 tbls. olive oil

5 garlic cloves, sliced

1 onion, minced

¾ lb. mild, dry sausage,
     thinly sliced

1 cup dry white wine or
     chicken stock

1 tbl. tomato paste

1 cup fresh or frozen tiny peas

    salt and pepper to taste

Place the eggs in a saucepan and cover with cold water. Bring to a boil, lower the heat and cook for 5 minutes. Remove from the heat, pour off the hot water and cover with cold water.

Meanwhile, heat the oil in a skillet. Cook the garlic over medium heat until golden. Add the onion and cook until soft. Add the sausage and cook for 3 minutes. Stir in the wine or stock and tomato paste. Cook until the sauce begins to thicken.

Peel the eggs and add them to the sauce. Cook for about 5 minutes. Cut the eggs in half and baste with the sauce. Sprinkle with the peas. Cook for a few more minutes until the peas are hot. Season with salt and pepper. Serve immediately with the sauce.

SPANISH STYLE RICE
SPANISH

1 ½ cups minute rice or cooked
       rice

16 ozs. tomato sauce

½ cup water

⅓ cup green pepper, diced

⅓ cup hot red or yellow
      peppers, diced

1 tsp. salt

½ tsp. prepared mustard

    dash black pepper

Combine all in saucepan. Cook about 1 hour. Stir in rice. Cook about 20 minutes. Let stand 5 minutes.

Serve with small, cooked pieces of beef or pork on top.

Alice Manfredi, West Mifflin

HOMEMADE TOMATO DUMPLING SOUP

large can tomato juice	2 cups flour
2 qts. water	1 tsp. salt
1 tsp. salt	3 tbls. shortening
1 tsp. sugar	1/2 cup flour
4 eggs	1 small onion, diced

Empty a large can of tomato juice into a 4 qt. soup pot. Put in 2 qts. of water, bring to a boil and add sugar.

Break eggs into bowl, add flour and salt and mix by spoon until thick. When tomato water begins to boil, add dumplings by teaspoonful. Each time dip spoon in the tomato water. Keep water boiling for 5 minutes after all dumplings have been added. While dumplings are boiling, put shortening and flour in frying pan and mix until brown. Add onion and let cook for 5 minutes then pour into tomato soup. Let cook for 1/2 hour.

TURKEY AND MACARONI CASSEROLE

3 tbls. butter	1 8 oz. can sliced mushrooms,
3 tbls. flour	reserve liquid
1 cup chicken stock	salt and pepper to taste
1/2 cup light cream	8 oz. macaroni
2 cups turkey,	1/2 cup grated cheese
cooked and coarsely cut	butter for dotting

Melt the butter and stir in flour smoothly. Cook, stirring constantly, for a couple of minutes. Add chicken stock, liquid from the mushrooms, and light cream and cook, stirring constantly until thickened and smooth. Add turkey and mushrooms. Season to taste with salt and pepper. Meantime, cook macaroni in boiling salted water 9 minutes and drain well. Line a casserole with the macaroni. Pour the turkey mixture into the center. Sprinkle cheese over and dot with butter. You may use any cheese you like — Cheddar or Parmesan are both good. Bake in 375° oven until golden brown, about 30 minutes. Serves 4.

CITY CHICKEN

1 lb. veal, cubed	salt and pepper
1 lb. pork, cubed	6 wooden skewers
bread crumbs	1/4 cup fat
1 egg, slightly beaten with	
1 tbl. water	

Alternate veal and pork cubes on stick. Mix together egg, water and salt and pepper. Dip sticks of meat in crumbs, then in egg and again in crumbs. Brown on all sides in hot fat in heavy skillet over medium heat. Season. Add a little water. Cover and cook over low heat or in moderate over at 350° for 1 hour. Serves 6.

CHOCOLATE COOKIES

1/4 cup butter	1 3/4 cups sifted flour
1/4 cup shortening	1/2 tsp. soda
3/4 cup sugar	1/2 tsp. salt
1 egg	1/2 cup milk
2 1 oz. bars unsweetened	1/2 cup chopped nuts
chocolate, melted	

Cream butter, shortening and sugar. Add one egg and stir in unsweetened chocolate. Add flour, soda and salt. Then add milk and chopped nuts. Bake at 400° for 8 to 10 minutes. Yields 4 dozen.

SPICED ICE-BOX COOKIES

1 2/3 cups sifted flour	1 egg, unbeaten
3/4 tsp. baking powder	1 tsp. vanilla
1/2 tsp. salt	1/2 cup soft shortening
1/2 tsp. cinnamon	2 tbls. milk
1 1/2 tsps. cloves	3/4 cup chopped nut meats
3/4 cup brown sugar	

Sift first 5 ingredients into a large bowl. Add remaining ingredients and mix thoroughly. Shape into rolls in waxed paper. Chill until hard enough to slice. Can be overnight. Bake on ungreased cookie sheet in 400° oven for 10 to 12 minutes. Yields 4 dozen.

CHERRY PUDDING

1 ½ cups sifted flour	1 tsp. vanilla
1 ½ tsps baking powder	¾ cup sugar
¼ tsp. salt	1 #2 can sour red pitted cher-
½ cup shortening	ries, including juice
1 cup sugar	½ cup boiling water
1 egg	

Resift first 3 ingredients twice. Cream shortening and 1 cup sugar until light and fluffy. Beat in egg and stir in vanilla. Add sifted ingredients a little at a time, beating well after each addition. Pour into a buttered 9" square pan 2 ½" deep.

Prepare sauce by heating ¾ cup sugar, cherries, juice and boiling water, and pour over batter. Place in a 350° oven and bake 45 to 55 minutes, or until pudding begins to shrink from sides and top is golden brown. When baked, sauce will be on bottom. Serves 8.

CINNAMON COFFEECAKE

½ cup butter (1 stick)	1 tsp. baking soda
1 cup granulated sugar	1 cup dairy sour cream
2 eggs	¼ cup light brown sugar,
1 tsp. vanilla	firmly packed
¼ tsp. lemon juice	1 tbl. granulated sugar
2 cups sifted flour	1 ½ tsps. cinnamon
1 tsp. baking powder	¼ cup chopped nuts

Generously butter a scalloped pan, 7 cup or 10". In mixing bowl, cream together butter and sugar until light and fluffy. Add eggs one at a time, beating well after each addition. Blend in vanilla and lemon juice. Sift together flour, baking powder and baking soda. Add to creamed mixture alternately with sour cream beginning and ending with dry ingredients. In a small mixing bowl blend last 4 ingredients.

Pour half the batter into pan and sprinkle brown sugar mixture over batter. Pour in remainder of batter. Bake in preheated oven for 45 to 50 minutes. Let cool 10 minutes on wire rack then carefully remove from pan. Serve warm. When using tube pan, cake will bake to fill ½ the pan.

CHEESE CAKE

1 lb. cream cheese	3 tbls. corn starch
1 lb. cottage cheese	3 tbls. flour
1 1/2 cups sugar	1 tsp. vanilla
4 eggs	1/2 lemon, juice only
1/4 lb. butter or margarine, melted	1 pt. sour cream

Mix cream cheese and cottage cheese and add sugar. Add eggs one at a time and the next 5 ingredients. Mix thoroughly then add sour cream. Bake at 325° for 1 hour. Turn off oven and leave in oven for 2 hours. Remove from oven and put in cool place for 24 hours.

Hints: Use a 9" sponge cake pan and spray with a non-stick spray. Place graham cracker crumbs in bottom of pan so that the crackers will be on the top of the cake. If desired, add a can of crushed pineapple on top of the crumbs, then the batter.

CANDIED FRUIT CAKE

21 3/4 oz. dates	1/2 tsp. salt
1 lb. candied pineapple	1 cup sugar
1 lb. whole candied cherries	4 eggs
2 cups sifted flour	8 cups pecan halves
2 tsps. baking powder	

Cut dates and pineapple coarsely. Add whole cherries.

Sift flour, salt and baking powder over fruit and mix well separating pieces so they are well coated. Beat eggs until frothy. Gradually add sugar beating well to blend. Add to fruit and mix with large spoon. Add nuts and mix by hand until nuts are evenly coated with batter.

Press by hand into two 9" x 5" x 3" loaf pans that have been greased then lined with brown paper and paper greased also. Decorate. Bake at 275° for 1 1/2 hours. Leave in pans on rack for 5 minutes before removing paper. Double wrap with foil. When sliced, the slices resemble stained glass windows.

To bake 4 small cakes (7 1/2" pans) 1 1/4 hours.

Dolores M. Zewe, Duquesne

BLUEBERRY KUCHEN

1 ½ cups flour, sifted

2 ½ tsps. baking powder

2 ½ tsps. salt

1 egg

½ cup sugar

¼ cup milk

¼ cup melted butter or margarine

2 cups blueberries, washed and drained

⅓ cup confectioners sugar

Sift together the first 3 ingredients. Beat egg until light and gradually add sugar, milk and melted butter. Mix well then add dry ingredients blending well. Turn into a well greased 8" pan. Spread blueberries over dough and sprinkle with sugar. Bake at 350° for 40 minutes.

MOM'S LIME PIE

2 eggs

½ cup sugar

½ cup corn syrup

1 cup canned milk

1 cup milk

1 tsp. lime peel

⅓ cup lime juice

green food coloring

Beat eggs, add sugar gradually while beating. Stir in the rest of the ingredients and enough green food coloring to make a nice lime color. Put in a shallow pan and freeze until firm. Break up mixture into a chilled bowl and beat until light and creamy. Pour into 9" crumb crust and freeze until firm.

Crumb Crust

4 tbls. butter

1 ½ cups graham cracker crumbs, about 18 crackers

¼ cup powdered sugar

¼ tsp. nutmeg

¼ tsp. cinnamon

Melt butter, then mix all ingredients together reserving 1 tbl. to sprinkle on top, before freezing.

Pat Sommers, Munhall

NOTES

NOTES

GENERAL INDEX

Jam: 161

Jelly: 18, 52, 82, 117

Juice: 14-15, 17-18, 39, 44, 46, 54, 70, 79-80, 91, 110, 121-122, 128, 140, 147-148, 150, 161, 170, 172-174

Kale: 76

Kielbasi: 144

Kolbassi: 107, 113-114, 166

Lamb: 38, 42, 45, 97, 123-124, 149

Leeks: 99, 149

Left-overs: 76, 80, 126, 130, 136, 159, 163

Lemonade: 18, 161

Lentils: 22, 68

Lettuce: 11, 60, 87, 122, 161

Light-bread: 85

Lima beans: 108, 127

Macaroni: 122, 132, 170

Madeira: 149

Marshmallow: 167

Meat: 12, 21-23, 25-26, 33, 35, 38, 45-47, 49, 55-56, 58, 71, 91-92, 96-97, 101, 113-115, 124-125, 131, 133-134, 144, 149, 152, 163-164, 171

Meatballs: 133, 159

Meatless: 70

Meatloaf: 107

Meringue: 18, 128

Mint: 39, 97

Molasses: 14, 27, 35, 65-66, 79

Mousse: 87

Mozzarella: 136, 138

Muffins: 166

Mushrooms: 32-33, 45, 49, 82, 110-112, 137, 144, 149, 170

Noodles: 45, 55, 57-58, 125, 135-136, 140

Nuts: 8, 27-28, 42, 50, 61-62, 66, 78, 82-83, 98, 108, 131, 142, 145, 150, 153, 164, 171-173

Oatmeal: 47, 69

Omelet: 8-9, 161

Oranges: 15, 18, 79, 85, 140, 153, 161

Oxtails: 57

Oysters: 12, 17, 70, 162

Pancakes: 23, 32, 48, 69, 107, 117, 138

Parsnip: 70, 149

Paska: 42-43, 52

Pasta: 133

Pastry: 13, 16, 33-34, 46, 69, 72, 99

Peaches: 18, 71, 128, 149, 161

Peanuts: 32, 40, 78, 167

Pears: 21

Peas: 33, 39, 121, 125, 127, 131, 163, 169

Pecans: 82, 173

Peppers: 60, 92, 96, 139, 158, 169

Pheasant: 144, 149

Piecrust: 163

Pies: 12-13, 16, 18, 28, 33-34, 62, 68, 70-71, 80, 83, 92, 116, 118, 128, 136, 150, 163, 174

Pike: 148, 152

Pineapple: 62, 78, 80, 116, 140, 173

Plums: 62, 136, 139

Poppyseed: 108

Pork: 12, 20, 24, 32, 42, 47, 55, 76, 105, 114-115, 120-121, 124-125, 149, 169, 171

Potatoes: 9-10, 22-24, 33, 35-38, 44-45, 53-54, 57, 59, 62, 68, 70-71, 78-80, 107, 110, 112, 115, 120, 126, 134, 137, 144, 149, 153, 159, 163

Poultry: 26, 57, 149

Preserves: 18, 62, 146

INDEX TO RECIPE

INDEX TO RECIPE

SELECTED BIBLIOGRAPHY

Altankov, Nikolay G., *Bulgarian-Americans*. Ragusan Press: Palo Alto, CA, 1979.

Bodnar, John; Simon, Roger and Weber, Michael P., *Lives of Their Own: Blacks, Italians and Poles in Pittsburgh, 1900-1960*. Illinois: University of Illinois Press.

Burgoyne, Arthur G., *The Homestead Strike of 1892*. Pittsburgh: University of Pittsburgh Press, 1979.

Byington, Margaret F., *Homestead: The Households of a Mill Town*. New York: Arno & the New York Times, 1969.

Davis, Jerome, *The Russian Immigrant*. New York: The MacMillan Company, 1922.

Dickerson, Dennis C, *Out of the Crucible: Black Steelworkers in Western Pennsylvania, 1875-1980*. New York: State University of New York Press, 1986.

Garland, Robert, *The Scotch-Irish in Western Pennsylvania*. Pittsburgh: The Historical Society of Western Pennsylvania, 1923.

Gottlieb, Peter, *Migration and Jobs: The New Black Workers in Pittsburgh, 1916-1930*. Pittsburgh: The Historical Society of Western Pennsylvania, Vol. 61, 1978.

Halish, Dr. Wasyl, *Ukrainians in Western Pennsylvania*. Pittsburgh: The Historical Society of Western Pennsylvania, Vol. 18, 1935.

Kleinberg, S.J., *The Shadow of the Mills: Working-Class Families in Pittsburgh, 1870-1907*. Pittsburgh: University of Pittsburgh Press, 1989.

Lorant, Stefan, *Pittsburgh: The Story of An American City*. Doubleday: New York, 1964.

Marchbin, Andrew A, *Hungarian Activities in Western Pennsylvania*. Pittsburgh: The Historical Society of Western Pennsylvania, Vol. 23, 1940.

Miner, Curtis and Roberts, Paul, *Engineering an Industrial Diaspora: Homestead, 1941*. Pittsburgh: The Historical Society of Western Pennsylvania, Pittsburgh History, Winter 1989.

Murdock, Frank R, *Some Aspects of Pittsburgh's Industrial Contribution to the World War*. Pittsburgh: The Historical Society of Western Pennsylvania, Vol. 4, 1921.

Nurigiani, Giorgio, *The Macedonian Genius Through the Centuries*. David Harvey Publishing: London, 1972.

Rosenberger, Homer T., *Migrations of the Pennsylvania Germans to Western Pennsylvania*. Pittsburgh: The Historical Society of Western Pennsylvania, Vol. 54, 1971.

Silverman, Myrna, *Strategies for Social Mobility: Family, Kinship and Ethnicity Within Jewish Families in Pittsburgh*. New York: AMS Press, 1982.

Swetnam, George, *Labor-Management Relations in Pennsylvania's Steel Industry, 1800-1959*. Pittsburgh: The Historical Society of Western Pennsylvania, October 1979.

Thomas, Clarke, *They Came to Pittsburgh.... Pittsburgh Post Gazette*: Pittsburgh, PA, 1983.

Walsh, Victor A., *Across "The Big Water": The Irish-Catholic Community of Mid-Nineteenth-Century Pittsburgh*. Pittsburgh: The Historical Society of Western Pennsylvania, Vol. 66, 1983.

OUT OF THIS KITCHEN

*a History of the Ethnic Groups
and Their Foods in the Steel Valley*

SECOND EDITION

ORDER FORM

If you have enjoyed our book and would like to order additional copies, please send the attached order form along with a check or money order payable to *Publassist.*

Name: _____

Address: _____

City: _____State: ____Zip Code: _____

And/or send as a gift to:

Name: _____

Address: _____

City: _____State: ____Zip Code: _____

Name: _____

Address: _____

City: _____State: ____Zip Code: _____

Number or Books _____X $15.00 .... _____

Pennsylvania residents add 6% State Sales Tax .... _____

Allegheny County residents add 1% County Sales Tax ..... _____

Please add $2.00 postage and packaging per book .... _____

TOTAL _____

Mail to: *Publassist*
1671 New Haven Avenue
Pittsburgh Pa 15216-1918

For additional information please call 412-343-9749.
Or, visit our website at http://www.publassist.com